Hindsight Being 20 20

Eli Kwake

Copyright © 2020 Eli Kwake

All rights reserved. This book or parts thereof may not be reproduced in any form, stored in any retrieval system, or transmitted in any form by any means—electronic, mechanical, photocopy, recording, or otherwise—without prior written permission of the publisher, except as provided by United States of America copyright law.

Any references to historical events, real people, or real places are used fictitiously. Other names, characters, places and events are products of the author's imagination, and any resemblances to actual events or places or persons, living or dead, is entirely coincidental.

First Printing 2021

Print ISBN: 9781955587020

www.elikwake.com

For Nana

Acknowledgments

No book is created in a vacuum, and this book is no exception.

Thank you, first and foremost, to Alex Kwake. You put up with me griping about these stories and poems for a year. You helped me keep my sanity. Thank you thank you thank you.

Thank you to Ghislaine and Ryan Phillips, for seeing the promise in the first drafts of a lot of these stories.

Thank you Sadie Keljikian for helping me hash out the order of these stories and poems.

Thank you to my friend and cohort, Xander Benette, for your lone camraderie during the Tuesday night write ins where I often was polishing one of these gems.

Thank you, ever and always, to Ruth Kwake. You're the best alpha reader ever, and the best mother-in-law I could ask for.

Table of Contents

Wolf_Moon

The_Seeds_of_Winter
Don't_Be_You
I_Broke_my_Heart_into_Pieces
Calling_My_Name

Snow_Moon

But_None_of_Them_Were_Mittens
You_Told_Yourself_Stories
The_Phone_Call
The_Baltic_Sea_In_Winter

Worm_Moon

Between_Heaven_and_Hell
Flash_in_the_Pan
They're_Not_It
Recovering

Pink_Moon

Blind_D&Dating
Love_is_a_Garden
Sestina
Feels_Fake

Table of Contents

Flower_Moon

The_Flowers_in_the_Sea
Imperfect
How_Do_I_Sing
The_Dawn

Strawberry_Moon

Up_Up_In_a_Tree
Polly Penelope Poly Panda and the Particularly Penetrative Party
I Have Read All the Posts On the Forum
Tribute

Buck_Moon

The_Door_of_Distant_Dreams
Three_Times_True
About_June
Weather_the_Storm

Sturgeon_Moon

The_Children_of_the_Sky
Heartstring
Gods_and_Angels
In_The_Dark

Table of Contents

Corn_Moon

The_Bargain
Goblin
The_Bridge_Of_Death
Hey_Siri

Harvest_Moon

The_Fae_Will_Take_Your_Name
Pants
Can_You_Recall
Face

Blue_Moon

Whats_in_a_Name
Can_I_Wear_A_Suit
I_Never_Heard_You_Say_It
Half_Jack

Beaver_Moon

The_Moon_and_the_Void
Sing_a_Song_of_Sunshine
How Do You Write What Can't Be Written
Heartbeat

Table of Contents

Cold_Moon

I'm_Sorry_My_Body

Grief

Yesterdays_Sorrow

In_Days_of_Auld_Lang_Syne

Wolf Moon

The Seeds of Winter

Hades took me from where I slept in the field that day and . . . That was it.

I've heard the stories of rape and ruin that mortals tell, but they're not true. He didn't hurt me. Three months later he was still waltzing around me, like he was more frightened of me than I was of him. He'd find me, wherever I was lost that day, and just . . . talk. While I was trying to find my way out all he did was try to talk to me. Not that I listened.

Then Zeus came for me, telling of the blight and plague my mother was causing above. Hades agreed to give me back, but only if I could resist the temptation of food.

I hadn't eaten anything for those three long months, of course. I knew the rules. I knew that to eat the food of the Underworld was to live there forever. I was starving, but I wanted to go home. I wanted my mother to nag at me and be overprotective. I wanted her stifling fields and gardens, with everything planted neatly in rows. No weeds or wild riots of flowers. I wanted to go back to the life I had hated only three months before.

Hades brought me to the exit of the Underworld, and there he paraded food before me. Every denizen of the Underworld, it seemed, was carrying something. I'd never seen or heard of some of those foods. Some I didn't want to know about, some still make my mouth water when I think about them. Endless tray after endless platter. For three days I stood there, refusing everything.

On the last day, at sunset, he was there. Hades himself, holding a simple bowl of pomegranate seeds for me. He was the last in line. He knelt before me, holding the bowl like he was a slave. Like he, the King of the Underworld, was somehow less than I was — and he offered me the seeds.

He stared up at me as he did, wordless, but that gaze spoke to me in ways that his words hadn't in those three long months. It told me more than the so-called garden he had built for me. It nagged at me more than my desire to go home. It held me more than Zeus' presence. It called me even more than the knowledge that the world above was dying for every moment I tarried in that place.

"Please," he was begging, although his lips never moved. "Please, I am so lonely here. Do not leave me."

I took the seeds.

I swore I would never go back, no matter what deal Zeus made after I ate those seeds. I went back to my Mother, to my stifling life, to the mortal world. I was so happy to be back. I dreaded going back to the dreary Underworld in six months. I was determined to enjoy the time I had at home.

I hated being home.

I thought Mother was restrictive and overbearing before Hades took me from the field. She had always chased away all of my suitors. But after she kept me at her side at all times. She slept in my room when I refused to sleep in hers. At first it was almost a comfort, a relief to have her there at night. But as the first week turned into the first month, I began to feel restless, almost itchy.

I was trapped in a golden cage of my mother's making, and I longed to be free.

One night, nearly two months after I returned home, I inched from my bed while Mother was sleeping. I crept back to the field Hades had stolen me from. It had always been my refuge when I was feeling restless. I had played there often as a small child. I had practiced my growing powers there. That field was home, more even than my mother's house and hearth. Not even what Hades had done could change that.

He was there, of course, waiting for me.

We stared at each other for a long time after I found him there. He stood very still, very straight as he watched me. Later he told me he was afraid to move, to even breathe, for fear that I would run from him. All I could think then was that he looked powerful. That day when he had knelt before me, begging me with his eyes to stay with him . . . it seemed years away.

He was darkness in the moonlight, and I could not have run from him if I tried.

After we had stood there too long, I shifted, uncomfortable. Dead fall under foot crackled, breaking the silence. The rustling of the leaves beneath my feet helped me find my voice.

"What are you doing here?" I asked.

He snapped his gaze away, as if I had slapped him. He looked out over the field. There had been flowers growing there before he took me. They had returned in a riot, thicker than before. It was as though the flowers were rejoicing in my return.

"I come here often," he said, his voice so quiet I had to strain to hear him. "I have been hoping to find you here again since you left me."

"Since I went home," I snapped back.

I folded my arms, trying to guard myself against the sudden flash of sorrow across his face. Almost before I was certain I'd seen it, he had reattained his neutral mask. He stared at me, then, for a long moment. He nodded to himself, as though deciding on something. He took a step closer to me, and then another when I did not back away.

"You don't remember, do you?" he asked, in that quiet voice of his. "When we first met."

I scowled. "It was shortly after you kidnapped me."

He only smiled and continued to walk slowly towards me, step by cautious step. "You were a very young child at the time. I estimate you were . . . perhaps four years old? You were here making flowers. You asked what I wanted. I told you nothing grew in the Underworld, and you gave me the first Asphodel flower."

I didn't remember.

"I suppose that's when you decided you were in love with me?" I asked, my voice dry.

He stopped only a few inches in front of me. I resisted the urge to back away. "No," he said. "I thought you were a sweet child, but that is all." He reached out and tucked a lock of my hair behind my ear. "I fell in love with you much later."

I slapped his hand away. "What you feel for me isn't love, Hades."

"Perhaps."

He grabbed the hand that had slapped his away, and kissed the palm tenderly. I felt . . . a jolt — a thrill, maybe — rush through me, and I pulled my hand away, uncomfortable. I tucked my hands behind me. What was wrong with me?

He sighed and started to turn away. "Go back to your mother, Persephone."

"Wait, I . . . " I reached out, unthinking, as he turned. He froze, before turning back to me. I opened my mouth to say something, but the sudden intensity of his gaze made the words die in my throat. I closed my mouth and swallowed hard. Before I knew what was happening he had crossed the distance between us. He covered my mouth with his.

Once, twice, three times he kissed me. One hand held mine, the other caressed my cheek lightly as he pulled away.

"Goodnight," he whispered, once again the darkness in the moonlight. I was frozen. "Until next we meet, my wife."

And then he was gone.

It was several days before I could convince myself that the encounter didn't mean anything. I told myself I was safe, that he wouldn't be there. I returned to the field, and he was waiting. He smiled when he saw me, and handed me a bouquet of Asphodel flowers. I scowled and threw them back in his face. He only laughed and kissed me again, once, twice, three times.

We met often, those next few months. Sometimes we

argued. Or, I would argue. He would never fight back. Sometimes we talked. Once we spent the whole night, almost until dawn, telling each other stories and making each other laugh. I learned more about Zeus and Mother than I had ever known. Always, he would kiss me three times. Sometimes it was when I had only just arrived, often when he was leaving. I told myself that I never kissed him back.

Some days, I even believed myself.

In my mother's home, things did not get better. I finally ejected her from my room after an argument that brought Zeus down to mediate. Still, she kept me close to her side by day. I was forced to work in the fields, helping to prepare for the harvest as the months ticked by to my eventual departure. By night I sought out Hades more and more often.

"You are a wild thing," he said when I complained about my mother's clinging to me for the hundredth time. "It's part of why I took you." He tucked my hair behind my ear again.

"You shouldn't have taken me at all," I grumbled, but my heart wasn't in it.

He chuckled. "I wanted to offer you your freedom in the Underworld. To rule it beside me as my Queen." He sighed. "Perhaps I was a little short sighted, kidnapping you. That was Zeus' idea."

I groaned. "Why would you ever listen to him?"

He smiled and leaned in close. "Because I am in love with you" he whispered, and then kissed me once, twice, three times, each kiss lingering longer than the last.

When he pulled away at last, I listened to an impulse. Before I knew what I was doing, I followed after him. I pressed a soft kiss to his lips, just once. Our eyes locked. He looked almost as startled as I felt. The silence between us almost crackled as I did not move away and he did not move back.

"Can I . . . ?" I asked, hesitantly moving towards him.

"Yes," he breathed, reaching back.

We met in the middle and fell together into the soft grass. For a long moment I stared at him — darkness in the moonlight — and he looked back at me. I wondered what he saw. And then we moved closer to each other, and there were other things to think about.

Dawn saw me trudging back to my mother's house. She caught me sneaking in the window. It was . . . not one of our better days as mother and daughter. It was still a month until I was due to return to the Underworld, to Hades. She forbade me to leave the house and assigned three nymphs to watch me at all times. I raged and cried for a full day. Then I was numb, dying to get outside. I was trapped again, and this time there would be no escape for me.

It was at the end of the first week that I began dreaming.

Hindsight

They were little dreams at first. Hades holding my hand. Tucking my hair behind my ear. Smiling at me when I'd said something nasty to him.

At the end of the second week they changed. Hades caressing my cheek. Holding me against him. Kissing my palm.

At the end of the third week they changed again. Every kiss. Every touch. Every smile. I remembered it all in dreams. Those three kisses felt engraved on my lips. It felt almost like he had been casting a spell over me, but the only spell was in my mind, on my heart. I was full of a longing that rivaled even my desire to be free. I wanted him. I wanted Hades.

The end of my time with Mother arrived, and still she would not let me go. Zeus came to escort me, but she refused him. A week went by. I ate little and slept less. I felt as though I was dying. I didn't know what was wrong with me. I found myself crying often, silently weeping tears of misery and sorrow. Mother was convinced they were tears of relief.

At last, Hades himself came to collect me from my mother's house. I watched from the doorway, feeling unsteady on my feet, as he approached Mother in the garden. One of the nymphs tried to usher me inside, and I shook her off.

"You dare," my mother hissed at Hades as he stood before her, unflinching.

"Demeter, she is my wife," he told her reasonably.

She slapped him. "She is my daughter first!"

Hades saw me, then, watching them. I was torn between my duty as a daughter and love for my mother, and what I had only just started to realize was love for my husband. He took a step towards me, a hand outstretched.

"Persephone," he said in that quiet way of his. "Come with me."

My vision wavered, and I saw two of him. One stood with his hand outstretched. The other knelt, offering me the tray of pomegranate seeds. *Please. I am so lonely.* My vision wavered again, and I saw darkness in the moonlight. *I come here often.* Those three kisses against my lips, sense memory. *Because I am in love with you.* I clutched at my head and at the doorway, and my vision cleared.

"No!" Mother stepped between us, her hands spread wide, as though she could keep us apart by sheer force of will.

But I already knew what I had to do.

I moved forward, out of the doorway, and placed my hands on my mother's shoulders. "Mother," I told her gently, quietly. "I love you. I promise I will return."

And then I stepped around her and into the waiting arms of my husband.

Hindsight

Don't Be You

You can be anything you want to, a singer, a writer, a cook
Just don't be you
You can listen to music, oldies, classical, or rock
Just don't be you
You can only be happy, push past the fear
And don't be you
Stop climbing trees, start wearing skirts
And don't be you
We don't understand how you can be so selfish
Why are you you?
You're not choosing a side, you're not trying to hide
Why are you you?
Hide away your heart, never mind what you want
Just stop being you
Can't you see it's too late for you to be yourself?
Just stop being you

All we ever wanted was for you to be a doll
All we ever asked for was don't be you at all

I Broke My Heart Into Pieces

I broke my heart into pieces
I hurt my soul quite a bit
I shattered my home and my hearthstone
I thought, for the fun of it

I picked a fight with you, lover
I told you that you weren't enough
I wanted to feel something true, something real
I needed to know I was tough

Now I am waiting in ashes
The smoke and flames I create
Burn all around me from bridges I've burned
Now here, in the ashes, I wait

I'm sorry for what I have spoken
I'm sorry for what I've not said
I'm sorry for burning the bridges to you
I'm sorry for what's in my head

I know I will never be prefect
I know that you need more than me
I know you are broken and breaking
I know you should move on, you see

Never mind my soul, how it shatters
Never mind what I've done to my heart
I would rather see you be happy with someone
Than stay here to be torn apart

Hindsight

I am the monster inside me
I am the beast at my door
I will break myself into pieces again
Scattered all over the floor

But somehow you still will not leave me
Somehow you walk through the flame
Burned as we both are by what I have said
Still you are here all the same

Slowly we pick up the pieces
Your heart, it is somehow intact
I love you more with the pieces we find
I love you, and that is a fact

I know that you deserve better
I know I am falling apart
But you help put me back together again
And together, we make a new start

Calling My Name

I grew in a land where the winds blew wild
Pushing and pulling and calling my name
Out through the doorway and into the desert
To run through the sands and was ever the same

Now I am grown and I live somewhere tamer
Where everything moves at a more sedate pace
The winds do not scream and the sands do not blow
And I'm not as wild, and wear a calm face

Sometimes I long for the child who's running
Free with the wind in their tangle of hair
Sometimes I think I am better far from it
Free to become who I am, far from there

Sometimes the wind howls as though it is searching
Sometimes I can hear it calling my name
Sometimes I think that I should be running
Wild with the wind, and was ever the same

I think I will always be pushing and pulling
Some part of me wild, some part of me tame
For I am the fickle breeze that is blowing
I am the thing that is calling my name

Snow Moon

But None of Them Were Mittens

A few weeks after Mittens died, Mom came into my room with a piece of newspaper in her hand.

"Jamie, what do you think about getting another cat?" she asked.

"I don't want to buy another cat," I answered glumly. "I want Mittens."

Mom knelt next to me and put a hand on my shoulder. "I know, honey," she told me, "but Mittens is gone. You can't have Mittens again. But we wouldn't be buying one, we would be adopting one. Maybe even two! You see?"

She held up the newspaper for me to look at. At the top of the paper in bold print were the words "Adoption Event Today!"

There were pictures of kittens and puppies, and a picture of the nearby pet store.

"I don't want to adopt a cat either," I grumbled.

"Why don't we at least go look and see what there is at the pet store?" Mom asked. "There will be lots of dogs and cats, and also fish and birds, and who knows, maybe even an alligator!"

"Okay, Mom," I agreed. Maybe it would be worth it if there was an alligator. Mom got her keys and we went to the pet store.

Outside of the pet store there were all kinds of dogs. There were big ones and small ones, shaggy ones and ones that had almost no hair. There were tiny cute puppies and big older dogs. But none of them were Mittens, and I wanted Mittens.

"Let's go inside," Mom said.

Inside the store, at the very front, were dozens of kennels filled with kittens playing. They were all different colors. Some of the kennels had mother cats in with their kittens, looking regal and relaxed. But none of them were Mittens, and I wanted Mittens.

"Oh, look at the kittens!" Mom said, and went over to the kennels.

"Mom," I said, "what about the alligator?"

"Well, if you want to look further in, you can. I'll come find you in a few minutes, I just want to look. They're just so cute!"

I wandered further into the store to see what else there was. Mom had said there would be fish and birds, and I wanted to see if there really would be an alligator.

At the end of the row of cats was a woman with a cat in her lap. People went to see all of the other cats, but not to this one. I walked over to her. The cat in the woman's lap was a beautiful black cat, with sleek, shiny fur. She was purring as the woman pet her and looked sleepy.

"What's her name?" I asked the woman.

"This is Juniper," the woman said. "She's ten years old and her last owner died. None of his family wanted her."

"Can I hold her?" I asked.

"Of course."

The woman handed Juniper to me, and I pet her gently, just the way I used to pet Mittens. Juniper purred in my ear and rubbed her face against mine. She wasn't Mittens. But she was Juniper, and I liked her very much.

"There you are," Mom said. "Who did you find?"

"This is Juniper," I said, still holding the sweet, black cat. "She lost her owner, just like I lost Mittens."

"Did you want to adopt her?" Mom asked.

"Can we?" I turned to the woman who had been holding Juniper. "Is it okay if I adopt her?"

The woman smiled. "Would you like to?"

"I think I would."

Mom said, "What do you think of a kitten, too? There's one

I like."

"Okay, Mom."

I went with Mom and Juniper to find the kitten she wanted. We adopted Juniper and a little orange tabby kitten that Mom named Rupert. We took them home and Mom helped me introduce Juniper to Rupert. Juniper was very patient with him. Rupert liked to play with her tail. She would calmly put a paw on him and groom him when he got too wild.

I still miss Mittens. Mittens was a good cat. But I like Juniper, and I like Rupert too. Rupert likes to play. He's really funny. Juniper likes to snuggle and sleeps on my bed. She's very sweet.

I didn't want to adopt another cat, but Mom was right. I can't have Mittens again, but now I have Juniper and Rupert. Neither of them is Mittens, and that's okay. I love them just as much as I loved Mittens, but in new and different ways.

You Told Yourself Stories

<u>AN: this was written to be read at my grandmothers—my Nana's—memorial on February 27th, 2020. She passed on February 16th, 2020, at home and close to loving family.</u>

Before I wrote books, before I wrote song
I was a poet, have been all along
Do you remember that first scrap of verse?
Do I think rightly that it was the worst?

I told myself stories, in my head, in my mind
I saw them in visions, I heard them in rhyme
In the forest, the cabin, the desert, the sea
All of these stories lived inside of me

I burst at the seams and the stories fell out
Sometimes with a whisper, sometimes with a shout
Out through my pen, onto paper, in reams
Sometimes a writer can't help it, it seems

Sometimes you saw them, and then, sometimes, not
We baked, hiked, quilted, and painted a lot
You were an artist, a teacher, and then
Sometimes just my Nana, sometimes just my friend

I told you once of the stories I feel
And you told me then something true, something real
It changed how I saw things, my whole paradigm
You told yourself stories all of the time

Hindsight

You told yourself stories, and I have to know
Where did they come from? Where will they go?
Will they disappear and let this world be?
Or have you given some now to me?

Can I write down your stories, your poems, your songs?
Would it feel forced, or like it belongs?
Are they even something that I can tell?
There is the truth, the crack in the bell

The stories you told yourself, older and young
Are already written, some barely begun
The stories you told, they are here, in this room
We are your stories, fully in bloom

The Phone Call

She's gone now
ERROR: emotion not found
Dissociating
Not falling to the ground

I was awake
When your call came in
I knew to expect
The crying on your end

I don't know what to tell you
I don't know what to say
I'm not good at words
I'm not good at all today

The Baltic Sea In Winter

"How are you feeling?"
How do you think?
I haven't fallen
I'm doing just fine
But I'm kind of angry
And nothing feels real
Except when it does
Roiling up from the deep
Under still waters
Not tepid, but cold
Roiling, cold waves
Sudden and painful
Like stepping into
The Baltic Sea
In winter
As young as I seem
I am growing old
Old on the inside
Old on the out
And different there, too
I dyed my gray hair
I put on my suit
I left off my tie
I left my apartment
And I said goodbye
"How are you feeling?"
I do not know
I wish you would stop
Asking me that
Some days are better
Some days are worse
Sometimes I write stories
Sometimes I write verse

Hindsight

"How are you feeling?"
I guess kind of sad
I wish you'd stop asking
And let me move on
At my own pace
But thank you for checking
I know this is hard
It's different for everyone
But let me withdraw
I will grieve as it hits me
With ice and with pain
Over and over
Again and again
Like stepping into
The Baltic Sea
In Winter

Worm Moon

Between Heaven and Hell

Jamie tried to ignore the sounds of the screaming as they shuffled along in a line of the damned. They were damned, they knew. In hindsight, they even knew how and why, and that it was entirely their fault. If they had listened to their most recent mother, they would be ascending right now, rather than in a line waiting to be flung into a pit, or a void, or whatever, exactly, was about to happen.

Hell on Earth was, apparently, standing in a line for the rest of whatever.

There was still a lot of fighting going on, but they were doing their best to ignore it. Everyone knew that eventually there would be a winner, but in the meantime, they were either headed for damnation or eternity. And Jamie was headed for damnation, so . . . whatever.

"Hold on, you there!" a rough voice yelled. A pair of burning hands seized them, and they were forcibly wrenched around to face . . . well, probably a demon, based on the mottled gray green skin, the pointed ears and teeth, and the bat-like wings, but otherwise, they were kind of . . . cute? "You. You're kind of blurry. Show me your true form, mortal!"

They scoffed. "This *is* my true form. I was born in it, Crowley, and I'll be damned in it too."

Crowley narrowed their eyes. "You." He dragged them a few paces out of line. "I should have known. The King needs to see you, he's been looking for you everywhere!"

Before they could do more than squeak in protest, they found themself being scooped up in Crowley's arms. Crowley took a running start and in the next moment, they were flying at an incredible speed towards the Mountain. Jamie held on for dear life, trying not to scream. This was . . . not exactly the damnation they had been expecting.

The Mountain hadn't always been there. It had appeared somewhere around the same time as the seas boiling. It towered so far above the horizon that it was visible everywhere on this continent. A singular column of rock and dirt, like the Devil's Tower in Wyoming, but infinitely taller. They had wondered a few times if it actually *had been* the Devil's Tower, but the placement, they had decided, was probably wrong.

Crowley took them right to the top. There, waiting, were two thrones. One a void of infinite light. The other shone with profound darkness. Standing by the thrones were two figures. One, seemingly a human male, the other, an enormous demon twice the size of Crowley. He was beautiful and terrifying to behold.

It pissed Jamie off.

Crowley landed them, and set Jamie down. He knelt before the demon. "I have found her, my King."

"Excellent. You may return to your other duties."

Crowley nodded, and flew back down off the Mountain.

"Stop that," Jamie said, scowling at the demon. "You can save your illusions, King of Lies, because I can see right through you."

The illusion of the enormous, beautiful demon popped like a balloon, and standing in it's place was a man. Still beautiful, still shining darkly, but normal enough. Somehow he was still terrifying, but they ignored that. It couldn't be helped, after all. Jamie was just a mortal, and this was Lucifer.

The other man was also beautiful. Jamie knew a dozen names for Him, but they supposed YHWH would do. They had never been a fan of the other names for Him. Jesus, Christ, etc. It was all the same, and all stupid, and designed to engender awe and fear.

He, as far as Jamie was concerned, was no better than Lucifer, and worse, in some ways.

"What do you two want?" Jamie asked flatly. The two men looked at each other, surprised, and then back at Jamie.

"Well, you, of course," Lucifer said with a sly smile. "You started all this, and it is up to you to finish it."

They blinked. "You mean, after all this time, you're still fighting about *me*?"

YHWH nodded earnestly.

Jamie made a disgusted noise. "Boys, boys, will you please just *move on*? I assure you, I have."

"I made you for a purpose," YHWH said, frowning slightly. "And yet you chose *him*." He glanced sidelong at Lucifer.

They stared at Him, aghast. "I was *three hours old*. You were still creating stuff. How was I supposed to know not to talk to your brother? You certainly didn't *tell* me, and then you spent the next whatever *punishing* me for it!"

Lucifer grinned slyly. "We did more than just talk, as I recall. We could try it again, if you like."

Jamie gave him a flat look. "Don't even get me *started* on *you*, Lucifer."

YHWH stepped forward and took their hand. "You must

choose one of us, Lillith."

"It's Jamie now," Lucifer said, before they got the chance. He stepped forward and took their other hand. "He's right, though. All this fighting stops when you choose. You've stood beside me, in some lives. Beside Him, in others. Who's it's going to be, Jamie?"

They yanked their hands out of the grasp of the gods, and backed away. "Why should I choose between my abuser and the one who *let* me be abused?" they demanded coldly. "Don't think I don't remember every last minute of those lives."

"Lillith, you have to decide," YHWH said, reaching out a hand towards them.

"I don't *have* to do anything," they said bluntly, crossing their arms. "What's in it for me, anyway? You," they pointed at YHWH, "abused me for all of my lives. How many times was I burned at the stake, stoned to death, raped, murdered, martyred, and for what? Exercising the free will *you* instilled in me?"

"Good points, all," Lucifer pointed out.

"And *you*!" They pointed at him. "You are literally the king of lies. You stood aside as He did all that to me. You did *nothing*. And what will you do to me if I choose you, hmm? You think I don't *know* it will be as bad, if not worse, with you? And you took advantage of me when I was mere *hours* old!"

"But I never lied to you, in any of your lives, Jamie," Lucifer said quietly.

"Illusions don't count?" They snorted. "Pull the other one, it has bells on it."

"She's got you there," YHWH said.

"It's they," Jamie told Him coldly. "I use they them. You may have forced me to be female this time, but that doesn't mean I am one."

"You spent too much of your last life thinking," He grumbled.

Lucifer shook his head. "He won't listen. You know why you were damned, in your last life. You *chose*."

"Yeah," they said bluntly. "I denied *both* of you. Him because of His followers, you because you were you. I *still* deny you both."

Lucifer sidled up to them, and turned them so they were looking off the mountain. From here they could see the angels and the demons fighting, almost blacking out the sky. They wanted to break and run away, not to look, but Lucifer held them fast. He nuzzled Jamie's hair, and kissed their neck. They shivered involuntarily.

"Look at what you are creating, Jamie," he whispered, his lips brushing their ear. "All this fighting continues, forever and ever, for you."

They took a deep breath and elbowed him in the ribs. He released them, and Jamie stepped away and turned to face him and YHWH. As Lucifer re-straightened, Jamie scowled. When Lucifer and YHWH stepped towards them, they backed away until they felt the edge of the cliff. Jamie looked down at the distant ground and considered.

They looked at the two before them, and smiled. "You want me to choose between you and stop the fighting? I have some bad news for you. I have chosen, and it's not you."

And Jamie took another step back and plummeted backwards. They fell, and fell, and fell. They saw wings flying down to them, one shining dark and the other infinite light. Jamie closed their eyes. They searched within, and found what they were looking for. It was easy, like flicking a switch.

They spun as a burst of color bloomed from them. Just before they hit the ground they were gliding, then soaring upward and away from the idiots behind them. Jamie heard shouts, demands that they come back, and ignored it. If the boys wanted to talk, they could come and find them. They found an island. Just a small one, with a palm tree growing in the middle and a little scrub grass. They sat against the tree and waited, watching the fighting.

They could still stop it, they knew. They could go back and choose one of the flawed gods, and all the fighting would stop. Someone would be declared winner, and Heaven or Hell on Earth would begin. There didn't need to be anymore suffering.

As far as they were concerned, Hell was already on Earth, and had been since the dawn of time. How many people had they watched die? And all for what? So that those two could sit around bickering over who got to own Jamie? They closed their eyes for a moment and allowed a few tears to fall for all those wasted lives. Their own wasted lives and the lives of how many others? All for what?

Between Heaven and Hell . . . yeah, right . . .

"It's already Hell," they whispered to the fighting angels and demons far away in the sky. "It always has been. How can I choose when they chose for all of us?"

Flash in the Pan

Damned if I do
Damned if I don't
Hell if I will
Hell cause I won't

Like a clockwork running
The creeping sands of time
I just can't keep up
With my overactive mind

Damned if I don't
Damned if I do
Don't mind me
I'm just passing through

I'm a nothing no one
I'm the flash in the pan
Am I sun rising or setting?
Enjoy me while you can

I think my time is waning
And I'm not ready yet
Am I measured years or hours?
Have I started to set?

Hindsight

Can anybody hear me?
Am I screaming at the void?
Why do I even bother?
My future is destroyed

I'm a nothing no one
During the apocalypse
I'm not a sun that's rising
I'm a sun due for eclipse

They're Not It

It's the little things like
My watch going off repeatedly
I'm on the bus and
Someone's taking the seat next to me
Or they're biking on the sidewalk
Instead of in the street
They're texting on their phone
Instead of talking when we meet
It's someone talking behind me
About stupid things
Or maybe just not answering
Their phone when it rings

I know full well the reason
I am angry off and on
I know there is more coming
Because I know you're gone
It's nothing that they're doing
It's nothing that they are
It's the pain that I am feeling
The hurt turning to a scar
So as much as I do not want
To meditate and sit
I know why I am angry
And they're not it

Recovering

Light breaks through my window
Through the darkness in my mind
Wakes me from my slumber
For the waking world to find
Sunlight through the shadows
Of this tiny boxlike room
Coughing, sleeping, fearing
Will this place be my tomb?

Will I now infect him
The man who sleeps beside?
It's hard to run from this
When there's nowhere else to hide
Am I waxing? Waning?
And will I be okay?
I've made it through another night
Hello morning, hello day

And so I move by inches
From the shadows to the light
From the bed onto the doorstep
Into daylight from the night
Many fade around me
Many die and more will pass
But me, I think, as once before
"This trial is not my last"

Pink Moon

Blind D&Dating

"I'm getting too old for this," I muttered as I tried for the third time to tie my cravat.

Brun, perched on my bed, only rolled her eyes. "Zee, I'm older than you are, and I still go on dates. You're just too much of an introvert."

"You have two boyfriends, *and* a girlfriend!"

"Hey! Polyamory is a legitimate lifestyle, and it's *work*!" she said insistently.

I realized I had tied the cravat wrong, and started to untie it again. "How do people even wear these things?"

"They don't, usually. Not anymore"

I ripped the offending cloth from my neck. "Why didn't you

say something sooner?"

She only smiled at me impishly. "Well, you seemed so determined!" The doorbell rang. "Oh, they're here! Last one to the door has to wash the dishes!"

Brun leapt from the bed and ran from the room. I shot the mirror one last, frustrated look. I wore a gray button down shirt, and black slacks. Was that even the fashion anymore? It would have to do. I trudged from my safe, quiet room, and made my way to the foyer.

Brun was already lip locked with Joseph, her date for the evening, when I arrived. Joseph had the excuse of being young, only ninety-seven, and Brun was . . . well. She was Brun.

But there was another person in the foyer, an apparently young woman I had never seen before. She was lovely, with a heart shaped face, vibrant green eyes, and an amused smile on her lips. I cleared my throat. Brun made a rude gesture, Joseph ignored me, but the young woman turned.

"Hello, I am Zachariah Glas," I said formally, holding out a hand towards her. "I am pleased to make your acquaintance, Miss . . . ?"

"Oh, I'm Amanda Price." She took my hand and shook it. "It's nice to meet you."

"Brun hasn't told me much about you, Miss Price. You're a friend of Joseph?"

She nodded. "Just Amanda, please. I met Joseph a few months ago, and we've been bonding over our love of vampire novels. We were talking about the book Sunshine, and he said Brun's roommate was just like Constantine. I said I'd love to meet you, and . . . well, here I am, and here you are. You're not actually a vampire, are you?"

"Would it be bad if I was?"

She laughed. "No, just . . . potentially awkward."

"I see. Well, no. I'm a . . . it's complicated."

"Isn't it always?" she asked. "I'm actually—"

"Amanda, what do you want on your pizza?" Joseph interrupted, holding up his phone. "I'm buying."

"Well, what are my options?" she asked. She peered at the phone, and Brun dragged me away into the kitchen.

"Grab the beer out of the fridge, will you? What do you think?" she asked, reaching into the cupboard for glasses. I went to the fridge and opened it. I pulled out the box of assorted beer Brun had in there. I handed her the box before contemplating her second question.

"I think I will have a soda," I decided. I also pulled out the two liter bottle of Sprite.

"No, you dingus!" Brun hissed. "Of Amanda!"

"She seemed pleasant."

"Zee!"

I sighed and muttered, "She seems very young."

"Well, she is. Younger than Joseph."

I shot her a glare. "How much younger, Brun?" She cracked a beer and poured it into a glass, ignoring me. That had to mean Amanda was very young indeed, maybe even in her fifties . . .

"Pizza will be here in twenty minutes," Joseph announced from the doorway. "Hey, is that beer?"

An hour later we were full of pizza, and seated at the dining room table. The pizza boxes had been cleared away, and the dice had come out. I surveyed my unsuspecting victims from behind a cardboard screen. Amanda smiled at me innocently, and I knew I would enjoy crushing her spirit.

"You find yourselves standing at the doorway of a dilapidated, old tavern," I said ominously. "From the doorway, you can smell old beer, mold, and rot. Everything is covered in a thick layer of dust. What do you do?"

"I back away slowly," Joseph grumbled. "Nope nope nope."

"I also back away," Brun groaned. "I do *not* trust you."

"I open the door and roll perception," Amanda chirped brightly. There was a groan from the other two, and I smiled. She would never be able to perceive my--

"Nat twenty!" she crowed.

I frowned. "Roll to confirm?"

She rolled a dice. "Nineteen."

"*Somehow*," I grumbled, "you perceive a faint odor in the air and a thin, wispy cloud of gas just beyond the door."

"I back away slowly," she said firmly.

I shuffled my papers around behind my screen with a sigh, and then smiled again. "Roll initiative."

It took them two hours to defeat the skeletons I had just thrown at them. To my bitter disappointment, I rolled badly and wasn't able to kill or even critically injure any of their characters. I folded my papers up in my cardboard screen after the battle.

"Let's stop there for tonight," I said, and the other three let out a sigh of relief. Brun collected the character sheets and handed them to me.. I put them and my screen in a little box, along with my dice. When I looked up again, Brun and Joseph were gone, and I was alone with Amanda.

"That was fun!" she said cheerfully.

"It was," I admitted. "I haven't run a game in person in a long time. I've been running everything online for ages . . . it's easier to find players. Thank you for suggesting this." I heard a door open and close elsewhere in the house, and I flushed. "I think we have lost them for the evening."

"Oh? Oh! Oh . . . " We shared a slightly uncomfortable smile, and she stood. "I should probably go."

I stood also. "I will see you to your car."

"I walked," she said. "I'm about a mile and a half from

here."

"In that case, I will see you home," I said firmly. "It is late for a young woman to be walking alone."

She smiled. "Joseph was right. Just like Constantine. Alright, then. I'm over on Lincoln."

We walked out into the warm autumn night. For the first block or two we walked in silence. I caught her looking up at the stars through the trees. I was reminded of my first impression. She was lovely. And young, I reminded myself. And I had only agreed to this date to appease Brun.

"Where are you from, anyway?" she asked. "I've been trying to place that accent all night."

I hadn't realized I even still had an accent. "Scotland, a long time ago. And you?"

"Oh, I'm a local, born and raised. Have you eaten haggis, then?"

"Unfortunately."

She laughed. "You sound like you like it about as much as I like avocados."

"What's wrong with avocados?"

"They're slimy! Oh look!" She pointed up. "That's the space station! Did you ever want to be an astronaut? I did, but I have horrible motion sickness. So much for that."

"I've never seen the appeal of space travel," I admitted.

"But I was alive for the early days of aviation. It seemed terrifying."

"Definitely! But fascinating."

The sidewalk narrowed, and I moved to walk behind her as we went down a steep hill. At the bottom of the hill the sidewalk widened and I moved to walk beside her again. I tried to think of something to say. She was interesting, smart, and beautiful. And young, I reminded myself again. I looked up and saw we were approaching Lincoln.

"It's a left up here," she said. "Just a few more blocks. Thank you for walking me home."

"Of course." We turned onto Lincoln, and I wracked my brain, trying to think of something to say. Why was I so bad at this?

"I can almost hear you thinking over there," she said. "Just blurt it out already."

I sighed. "You're . . . you're very nice, Amanda. I am glad to have met you. May I have your phone number? I believe I would like to do this again."

She smiled up at me. "Sure! I'd love to have a regular gaming group again!" She pulled out her phone and stopped, then looked up. "Or . . . did you mean like . . . another date?"

I reached into my pocket and pulled out my phone also. I looked at the sleek, shiny smartphone in her hands, then at my older model flip phone.

"I think . . ." I started, and my words caught in my throat. "Amanda, this is very improper, and I apologize, but I must ask. How old are you?"

She blinked. "I'm thirty-seven. Why?"

I took a deep breath. "I will be three hundred years old in October."

"So? Brun is like four thousand or something."

"There is a sizable age gap between us. You don't even know what I am." I wished the voice of doom in my head would be quiet.

"You don't know what I am either. So we'll talk about it on our next date." She took my phone out of my hand and punched in a number. "Call me." She handed me back my phone, then ran up to a nearby apartment building and disappeared inside.

I stared after her, and then looked down at my phone. I listened to an impulse and dialed the number on my display. I listened to the phone ring.

"Hello?" her voice said.

"Hello. It's Zachariah. Is now too soon for that second date?" I heard her laugh and held my breath.

"Come on up."

Love is a Garden

Love is a garden, see how it grows?
Sometimes not neatly, sometimes in rows
Water it often, but not too much
Growing your love takes a delicate touch

Sometimes it's platonic, a love with no end
The love of a sibling, a parent, a friend,
Cherish this love, it will see you through
When trouble comes into the garden you grew

Sometimes it's romantic, sometimes it's intense
This kind of love doesn't make any sense
This love grows in tangles, sometimes it grows weeds
Sometimes it grows flowers, sometimes it bears seeds

Some loves are messy, some loves are neat
Some loves are a triumph, some loves, a defeat
Some loves are stable, some loves will not hold
Some loves are timid, some loves are bold

Some loves will save you, some loves make you cry
Some loves will mourn you, some loves will die
Every love matters, the big and the small
Just don't forget to water them all

Love is a garden, verdant and green
Don't try to hide it, it's meant to be seen
Love is important, let your love shine
Love is important, and you're one of mine

Sestina

I sit today at home
Between its narrow walls
Wishing I was in my garden
Hating my life
Tedium and conflict
But I'm safe

As long as I am safe
Trapped as I am at home
With the tedium and conflict
Between the narrow walls
At least I have my life
If not my garden

I could go to the garden
I know that it is safe
But I know it's not my life
But those next door at home
Just beyond the walls
And there's the conflict

As long as there is conflict
I do not have my garden
Only these narrow walls
I have to keep them safe
So I am home
But such is life

Hindsight

It's not much of a life
Tedium and conflict
But at least I have a home
And a garden
I have people to keep safe
Beyond these walls

While I'm clawing at the walls
A new beginning in my life
Begins while I am keeping others safe
Despite the tedium and conflict
And my longing for my garden
I'm learning to love my home

The walls of my home
Against the life near my garden
I will keep others safe, there is no more conflict

Feels Fake

Everything feels fake
Is any of this real?
Am I ever gonna grieve?
Am I ever gonna feel?

Is it my medication?
Or is it just my brain?
Why aren't my eyes burning?
I know that I'm in pain

Where is now is the drama?
The falling down to cry?
It's not like I am happy
Just listen to me sigh

But everything feels distant
Like a story or a dream
I wish that it would hit me
I almost want to scream

Am I'm doing this wrong?
And is this a mistake?
But I still can't help it
Cause everything feels fake

Flower Moon

The Flowers in the Sea

"If Adat goes to the land, he will die."

That's what the Wise One said, when my parents brought me before her. My parents were a little frantic about it. I wasn't allowed to know there even was a land until I was twelve, and only then because I saw it. I liked to explore the Nothing, the stretches of empty sea between our colony and the next, where there was very little life. One day I explored in what I thought was a different direction of the Nothing, and instead I saw the land.

My parents were furious, mostly with themselves, for letting me wander so far away from home. They told me then and there about the Wise One's prophecy. I vowed that night never to go again to the land. I wanted to live. I was curious, but I wasn't stupid.

Time passed, as it always does. I grew up. I wasn't expecting it, and neither was she, but I fell in love. The Sea Witch can cast many powerful spells, but I always say the most powerful one she ever cast was the one she cast over my heart. She hates it when I say that, but it's true. I told her about the Wise One's prophecy, and she gave me a potion to carry with me in case I was ever forced to go to the land. It would keep me alive, for a price. I would have to marry a landwalker by sunrise at the end of thirteen years. For that reason, the Sea Witch and I never married.

I was a soldier. Our colony was at peace with the surrounding colonies, thanks in small part to the Sea Witch living among us. Most of my days (and occasional nights) were spent patrolling for bandits and killer sharks. The former were dealt with swiftly and ruthlessly. The latter were discouraged from the area, and killed only if necessary. They weren't smart creatures, after all, and they are needed for the health of the sea.

I was on patrol when it happened. There was a storm above. I was surfacing for a better look when a small landwalker child, no more than five years old, fell into my arms. She must have been in a boat that capsized in the storm. Her hair was dark, her skin dusky. Her eyes were wide with fear. She opened her mouth and immediately began to choke on the sea brine.

I did not hesitate. She was only a child. The sea can be cruel and cold, but I am neither of these things. I popped open the potion that would allow me to live on the land, and pressed it to the child's mouth. If it would allow me to live on land, perhaps it would allow her to live in the sea?

Her legs fused together. They sprouted scales, pale as sand, and patterned with little pink things, like coral. Many years later she would tell me they were called "flowers." I carried her home to the Sea Witch. She would know what to do, what I had done.

As I passed into the colony I signed with my free hand to another soldier that there was an emergency. He would tell the Captain, and she would find someone to fill in for me. The girl was asleep, passed out. I carried her to our home, and into the Sea Witch's workshop. She was with someone, a client – something about true love? I laid the girl in one of the alcoves in the cave, and waited impatiently.

There's always a price for the Sea Witch's magic. A goal must be met, or else. My goal had been to marry a landwalker, or else turn into seafoam. It was a common price for merpeople, turning into seafoam. I didn't know what goal this landwalker child would have to try to reach, or what price she might have to pay, to live under the sea.

When the mermaid left with her potion, and knowledge of

the price that might need paying, the Sea Witch turned to me. "Who is this?" she signed to me.

"A landwalker child," I signed back. "I gave her my potion."

The Sea Witch nodded absently and went to look at the girl. She tested the girl's tail, arms, and checked her eyes. She looked at the new gills on the side of the girl's neck, and listened, for a moment, to the girl's chest. When she finished she went to a shelf in the workshop and took down a carved stone tablet. She looked it over as I waited impatiently, trying not to fidget.

Finally she turned back to me. "There is a price for all things," she signed to me.

I nodded. "I will pay it."

"You cannot." The signing took me by surprise.

"It was my potion," I signed back emphatically.

"If you want to pay a price, then you may choose to raise the child. But she must pay her own price."

"What is it?" I signed, thinking there might still be a way for me to pay it.

"She must marry a merperson in thirteen years, or she will turn into a colony of jellyfish."

I drifted to the sea floor beside the sleeping child. I looked at her. "She is so young," I signed to my love.

The Sea Witch touched my shoulder gently, understanding. "Children grow," she signed back.

We named her Se'Janna. We had to call her something, and we had no way to speak with her at first, until she learned to sign. Se'Janna was a good name for her, I thought, meaning "land and sea", specifically where the two meet. Se'Janna was frightened and confused at first. We tried to explain through hand motions, but there was no way to know if she understood.

She learned the basics of signing quickly, and soon we learned her landwalker name was Phoebe. It took longer to explain to her what had happened – the storm, her transformation - but we kept trying. We left out only the goal she must meet and the price she might pay. There would be time enough to explain when she was older. She chose to use the name we had given her. She kept her landwalker name just between us three, the child, the Sea Witch, and me.

The Sea Witch was right, as she usually is. Children grow. When Se'Janna was twelve years old, she would explore the edges of the Nothing, just like I had at her age. I waited for her to come back full of questions about the land. Other merchildren did. But she never asked.

"Se'Janna," I signed to her one day. "Why do you never ask to go back to the land?"

She shook her head. "I live here now." She smiled sweetly. "I have you, Father, and the Sea Witch, and I love the sea more than I loved the land. I do not want to go back."

I sat with her then, and told her about the goal she would have to meet, and the price she might have to pay, for the life I had given her. She looked frightened. Well, I had also been frightened, when my parents had told me about the Wise One's prophecy . . . I tried to reassure her there was plenty of time, but she seemed troubled.

"Do they have to be a merman?" she asked.

I smiled. "No." I signed. "Merman, mermaid, whoever makes you happy. That's all we want for you Se'Janna. To be happy, and alive."

She shrugged, looking uncomfortable. "What if I never want anyone that way, or no one wants me?"

I kissed her forehead and hugged her tight. "You are my beautiful, sweet child. Someone will love you. Still, I will talk to the Sea Witch. There may be another way."

There was another way. I did not tell Se'Janna about it. I thought, six years is a long time.

But she never showed any sign of interest in flirting with passing sailors, or with her mermaid and merman peers. She only seemed interested in exploring the Nothing. I did not understand it.

When she turned sixteen, I began to express my concern. "You're already sixteen," I would sign to her. "Time is running out. Surely there is someone? Grali, perhaps?"

Grali was a young merman who often accompanied her

home from the Nothing. He was going into soldier training and it was obvious, at least to me, that he was more than half in love with her.

But she only shook her head. "No. I want no one."

It wasn't for lack of attention. Grali was the tip of the iceberg. She had been a lovely child, and she grew more and more into a beauty as a teen. Mermen and mermaids alike flocked to her, trying to court her. She was as kind as she was beautiful, and hated to turn them away. She was also honest to a fault. If she felt nothing, she felt compelled to tell them.

When she turned seventeen and still showed no interest in anyone, I began to panic. "Pick a friend," I signed, begging. "I love you. Pick anyone."

"No," she signed back, looking resigned. "I can't. Father, I can't do it. I can't love someone like that. Not to pretend, and definitely not to marry."

"Not even to save your own life? Lie!" I signed furiously.

"No," she signed. "I can't." And she swam from the cave.

I didn't understand her reticence. Every time I brought it up, she said only that she couldn't feel that way for someone. I didn't understand. I tried taking her to other colonies. I had loved the Sea Witch at first sight. Maybe there would be someone elsewhere . . . ? But no. We returned from each trip no further along than we had been before.

With a month left before she was doomed to turn into jellyfish, I offered her all I had left. I offered myself. "I don't want you to die, Se'Janna," I tried to explain.

"No," she signed back. "I just can't. Not with you, not with anyone. I can't feel that way. Something is wrong with me, and I just can't."

I hugged her tightly before signing back, "Nothing is wrong with you, my precious daughter."

The day came. As though to mock me, it dawned bright and sunny. I took Se'Janna to the land nearest where I had found her. She didn't understand why, but she came with me. We went up to the surface, not far from the beach. Near enough for her to swim. I looked at the beach, and sighed.

I had been so sure it would never come to this. I had sworn, fifty some years before, never to go to the land. But here I was. I took the knife from my side, and handed it to Se'Janna. She took it, confused.

"Kill me," I said in the landwalker tongue. "There isn't much time, only until sunset. I don't understand why you couldn't marry anyone, Se'Janna, but I respect your wishes and feelings."

She looked horrified. "No. No," she whispered.

"You asked me once if there was another way. This is it. You became a mermaid because of me. If you kill me, you will be a landwalker again."

"No," she said firmly, and dropped the knife into the water. "Never."

I dove down and brought the knife back up to the surface.

"Please." I could see the sun sinking toward the horizon. It had to be now. "I'm supposed to die when I go to the land. I've lived a good life, Se'Janna. I'm here at the land for you. I'm supposed to die, and you are supposed to live. I can't do this for you."

She smiled a pure, joyful smile. "Then live, Father. Live, adopt more children, save them, and show them the love and caring kindness you've shown me." She looked over at the sun. It was a bare sliver above the sea. "Live, and thank you for the extra years of my life. I love you, and the Sea Witch."

I took the knife and pressed it to my breastbone, and put her hand on the hilt. "Please," I begged.

Se'Janna tossed the knife into the sea again. "No."

And then the sun sank behind the waves.

I watched in fascinated horror and sorrow as my daughter, my Se'Janna, flew apart into thousands of tiny jellyfish. Each one with a tiny pink flower at their center. They floated around me, never touching me. I watched them for a long time, as the night fell around me. Pearls fell from my eyes into the sea, the tears of a merman. I felt as though I would surely die, surrounded there by the jellyfish that had been my daughter.

But I lived.

Eventually, I found the strength to go home.

It took years, but eventually the pain of losing Se'Janna was far enough away for me to think of adopting another child. I found him bruised, crying, and alone on a sea cliff. I had been spending more and more time near the land. I offered him the potion, telling him the price he might have to pay upfront. He came home with me. Adrian was seven, and had been abused by his father. He married a mermaid who loved him dearly when he was eighteen.

He was the first of many children I found that way. Abused, lost to the sea, abandoned, I gave them the potion, and took them home. All of them found love eventually. I never lost another child to the jellyfish. The children began to tell me they had heard of me, the merperson who would take any child to live in the sea. Others began to do as I did, bringing landwalker children to live in the sea. They lived, they loved, they thrived. We took what the land did not want, and found it good.

Sometimes, as the years wore on, I would see one, a jellyfish with a pink flower, and know that part of my Se'Janna was still out there, still alive.

Imperfect

I wish I could write a song of joy and happiness
Where everything is perfect, but I can't, I guess
Maybe it's because I do not like that kind of song
But what is happiness if nothing goes wrong?

There's shadows in the sunlight, there's stars out at night
When everything is wrong, there's something going right
When everything is fine, there is something going wrong
There's sorrow in the joy of every happy song

Every time I smile I know that it will pass
And every time I cry, I know that it won't last
There's smiles in my future, and I hope there are a lot
One for every tear I'll shed, for this sorrow that I've got

I'm sorry I'm depressing, I'm trying not to be
Hope is so hard when there's only sorrow to see
I know that somehow, someday, everything will turn out right
Even now in darkness, I'm reaching for the light

Life is what you make it, and it will be okay
Maybe not tomorrow, but on some other day
Even as I hate the pain and sorrow and strife
I love the light and shadows of my imperfect life

How Do I Sing

I don't know how to write this song
When everything I do, I'm doing it wrong
It doesn't really matter, what I do or what I say
They just kept telling me to go away

When everything is fading to the black
How do I know if my song will come back?

I don't know how to sing, I don't know how to write
My world has lost a guiding light
I'm lost in dark and silence and I do not know
How do you sing when the words won't go?

The Dawn

Awake again at dawn
The singing of the birds
The waiting for the call
That has come

The tears behind my eyes
Still they will not fall
I am empty, I am broken,
I am numb

Someday this will heal
Someday I will cry
Instead of lying, dry-eyed
In the dark

For now I only wait
With the morning
With the dawn
With the knowledge
With the memory
With the pain

With the hurting
Through the numb
With the waking
From the sleeping
With the future
Without you

You are gone

Hindsight

But at least there are birds
And at least I have words
And I know I will heal
Yes, that knowledge is real

But for now it is dawn
And I know you are gone
I'm awake and in pain
And I will be again

There are shadows
There is doubt
There is loss
In the dawn

But at least there are birds
And today I have words
I still know I will heal
Yes, I know that is real

Even now,
With the pain
In the dawn

Strawberry Moon

Up, Up in a Tree

"If you want me, come and get me," Crisscross panted from their perch in the tree.

Noire paused his flight just before them, languidly sweeping a hand up and under their chin. He leaned in closer. "Want you in which way, darling? Don't get me wrong, both involve ropes, but it's an important distinction to make before we proceed."

They tried to pull away, nearly falling off the branch in the process.

"I— I— You— You were dating Black Star . . . ?" they sputtered.

Noire tilted his head in contemplation as he released Crisscross's chin. "Was I . . . ?" he mused "Oh. yes. That was three weeks ago. Black Star has a lovely body and a wicked mind, but we just didn't have the right chemistry. You, on the other hand . . . "

"I'm not a girl!" they objected.

Noire shrugged. "Who said you had to be?"

"I'm not a boy either!"

He only chuckled, flying back a pace. "Really now, Crisscross, that doesn't matter to me! I'm wounded! But if you'd rather not give it a go, I could just kill you now . . . " A glowing orb of energy started to swirl above his hand.

Crisscross eyed the orb, thinking carefully about their predicament. They were in a tree, and unlike Noire, they couldn't fly. They were tired and bruised from the fight already. They didn't really have any way to dodge the attack except to jump thirty feet down, and that would be killer on their knees.

"What exactly did you have in mind? Skip the ropes for now, just . . ." they paused. "Look, can we start by talking and figure it out later?"

The ominously glowing orb disappeared with a small pop as Noire smiled. "Why of course, darling. You're right. We should really have a first date before we bring out the ropes. Would you like to get down out of that tree? I know a little coffee shop not far from here where we can sit and talk."

"The tree is fine for right now." They squeaked, clutching at the trunk of said tree as they wobbled and almost fell again.

Noire sighed. "If you insist. But I must insist on stabilizing your perch there." Before they knew what was happening he had flown forward to sit next to them, and had an arm around their shoulders. "Now, where should we start?"

Crisscross shrugged, trying to think. They could only think of one question . . . but it was an important one. "Why do you keep robbing banks?"

Noire smiled slyly. "Well, it tends to attract you superhero types and you're all a solid ten. Prime spank bank material." He paused, seeming to consider as Crisscross sputtered and flushed. "And the money doesn't hurt anything, either."

"You think I'm a ten?" they asked, irritated. "What are you, then, an eleven?"

He laughed. "I'm flattered. I had no idea you thought I was so attractive."

"I mean, I need glasses, but I'm not that short sighted."

Noire looked interested. "Really? How do you get away without them in costume?"

"Oh, uh . . . " They shook their head, trying to clear it. "I just don't wear them. My vision isn't that bad, just makes things a bit fuzzy when they're more than five feet away from me."

"Is that why you tend to run in with your little knives first and ask questions later?" he asked a little too idly.

Crisscross sighed. "Did you hear that argument I had with

Dragonloom last week too?"

Noire snorted. "I think half the city heard about that, and the other half will by next Wednesday."

Crisscross groaned. "When the Rockdale Gazette comes out. Thanks for reminding me." They thought for a moment, and then asked, almost afraid of the answer, "Do you ever wish you could . . . I don't know. Just stop? Hang up your cape, not be a superhero or a villain and just not use your powers except privately? Get out of the life, I guess?"

Noire seemed to think about this. They sat together in silence for a long moment. Crisscross had to admit, it was nicer in the tree with his arm around their shoulders, stabilizing them. He was warm, it was a little cool, and as long as they didn't look down, it wasn't too bad. Even if he *was* a super villain.

"I do think sometimes it might be nice to retire . . . " he said finally. "It's a young man's game, being a super villain., and I am getting older. But what would I retire to, my day job? I mostly see old people and children, so few people my own age."

"What do you—" They stopped and flushed. "I'm sorry, that's . . . never mind. I forgot, we're . . . sort of enemies? I'm not sure what we are trying to be right now, to be honest, but . . . "

"Let's start with 'attracted to each other' and take it from there." Noire said quietly. "I have no qualms about telling you I am an optometrist when I'm not robbing banks to entice attractive young superheroes like yourself to try and beat me up."

They looked at him, suspicious. "What is this, like a fetish thing?"

He tisked. "No kink shaming. It's not very polite."

Crisscross held up a hand. "Wait, wait. So when you said ropes would be involved . . . you meant you wanted me to tie you up?"

Noire smiled, cheshire-like. "Not necessarily. I'm a switch."

"A swi—" They stopped again. "Oh my god, you're actually seriously kinky, aren't you?"

He sighed. "I'd really rather talk to you about this at that coffee shop."

"I'm not going to a coffee shop in costume with a super villain.," they said decisively. "Are you kidding me? Dragonloom gets on my case enough as it is."

"Dragonloom is a jerk," he told them flatly. "Even the League of Super villains don't treat each other the way Dragonloom treats his teammates."

Crisscross mumbled something to themself, crossing their arms and shifting uncomfortably. They almost fell from the branch, but Noire caught them and helped them find their balance again. They glanced down at the ground below them, looming, and swallowed hard.

"What was that you were mumbling?" Noire asked.

"Nothing," they answered a little too quickly.

"Come now, Crisscross, we're just talking." His voice was gentle, teasing. "Who am I going to tell, Dragonloom?"

Crisscross sighed. "I'm not Dragonloom's teammate. I'm a probationary member of the team, but they can kick me off at any time and then the police will arrest me for vigilante justice if I try to fight crime anymore." They felt Noire's arm tighten around their shoulders and looked at him. "Is that not how it works with the League of Super villains?"

He smiled. "May I remind you, we *are* super villains? We don't exactly play by the rules. That's why we're the super villains."

"Right . . . " They looked away. "Look, maybe I should go. I really want to be a regular member for Dragonloom's team someday, and if anyone sees me up here with you . . . "

Noire removed his arm, and Crisscross found themself thinking how cold it was without it there. "I won't keep you. If you want to go, let us part on good terms, at least for the evening."

They looked down at the ground, feeling guilty, and then gulped.

"Well, what are you waiting for?" Noire asked.

". . . can you keep a secret?" they asked, nervous. "If we're parting on good terms?"

"I suppose, darling, but you're starting to ask favors at this point, and I might ask favors back," Noire drawled lazily.

Crisscross sighed. "I'm afraid of heights. I don't know what I was thinking of, climbing up here. I can't get down, and I'd really rather not get rescued by Dragonloom."

Noire blinked, and then smiled. "Oh. Well, now you're really asking favors, aren't you?"

"Look, are you going to help me or what?" they asked crossly.

"Oh, I'll help you, darling." Noire put his arm around their shoulders again. "For a price."

". . . what price?"

He leaned in close. "Let me buy you a coffee at that coffee shop I was telling you about earlier."

Crisscross sputtered. "What, in *costume*? Dragonloom will rip me a new one."

Noire snorted. "Like he did last week? Come on, you're already in the tabloids, darling, what's a little more gossip?"

They thought about this for a moment. A little more gossip might get them booted right off the team, and then what would they do? They loved fighting crime, it was their life.

But on the other hand . . . they really liked his arm around them. He seemed . . . nice. Not super villain-y at all, except maybe when he was flirting. He could have killed them six times already, and he hadn't. So maybe he was okay after all?

". . . alright," they agreed with a wince. "Dragonloom is

going to kill me, but alright. Let's give this date thing a try."

"With ropes?" Noire asked hopefully.

"Maybe let's just start with coffee."

Polly Penelope, Poly Panda, and the Particularly Penetrative Party

Polly Penelope, Poly Panda
Didn't want one single manda
She wanted them in twos and threes
In the bushes and the screes

The Zoo was safe but really boring
Instead of sexing, she was snoring
Given just a single mate
She didn't want to procreate

They tried to show her Panda porn
But she still felt quite forlorn
Wallowing with her panda friend
Eating, sleeping without end

Finally they brought more in
And then did the fun begin!
Fighting, sexing, pitching woo
She didn't really care with who

Two males fought an epic fight
Displayed for her all their might
She took the winner for her mate
The loser tried a different date

Elsewhere in the Zoo were cheers
Popping corks and cracking beers
And then some months later, maybe
Polly Penelope had a baby

I Have Read All the Posts On the Forum

I have read all the posts on the forum
There is nothing left now to read
Do I sit and wait?
Do I try to create?
Do I follow now, or do I lead?

There are rabbit holes that I can fall down
There are memories that I can chase
There are ones I can hold
If I'm feeling bold
There are some that I want to erase

There are stories that I could be telling
There are worlds that I want to explore
There are words in my head
There are books on my bed
There's so many and still I want more

But I've read all the posts on the forum
And still I am wishing for more
I should go and work
Instead of just lurk
Oh, look! A new unread! What for??

Tribute

I wrote a poem yesterday
I don't know how it went
I forgot to write it down
And now it's gone

I was in the bathtub
I had no pen or paper
No phone or tablet
Just my mind

So I'm sorry for this poem
Which doesn't even rhyme
Which I am now writing
As a replacement

Buck Moon

The Door of Distant Dreams

"They told me not to talk to you, not to even glance at you," said the girl with the wide green eyes as she sat staring at the wall, her arms around her knees. Her long brown hair fell nearly to her waist in loose straggles, tangled and knotted in places. Her hands and feet were filthy. It looked as if she had been walking and digging in black earth. "They said he would give you nightmares. They said that's not fair."

    The nurses had warned him she might be difficult, but he had a job to do. Still, he hated to see her in such a state. He pulled the hairbrush they had given him out of his bag and approached the corner where she sat curled. He knelt next to her. She turned away from him, moving her eyes to the other wall. It was a pity, he thought. She would have been pretty before . . . before whatever had happened to her and to her parents.

"My name is Doctor Laurence Jasper," he told her in a calm, soothing voice. "Would it be alright if I brushed your hair?"

"Oh, no, he wouldn't like that at all," she whispered.

"I'm sorry to say it's a mess," he tried again, a little more insistently this time. "I usually wouldn't offer, but they did ask me to try. I have a daughter around your age, so they thought I might be the best person to ask of all the doctors here. The nurses seem to be a bit afraid of you."

She stirred a little. She asked, still staring at the wall in front of her, "A doctor, you said?"

Perhaps he was getting somewhere. "Yes, I'm Doctor Jasper. I'm a psychiatrist. I'd like to help you, Abigail."

She continued to stare at the corner before her for a long while, her wide green eyes flicking back and forth as though reading words only she could see.

"It's too late, then," she whispered, at last, decisively. "Some of my dreams, I gather, were not dreams at all." She moved as if to touch her hair and stopped before speaking again in a normal tone. "And you have already . . . you've been here too long. He'll know you're here. You may as well."

It was hard for him to follow her. "I may as well . . . ?"

"My hair," she reminded him. "He won't like it, but perhaps

he will be lenient if I ask it of him. You're only doing your job, after all."

Unnerved, he hesitated, but picked up a matted lock of her hair and began to gently tease the knots out of it. Her hair was greasy, full of dirt and leaves, and it was slow going. They had been holding her for six days. He thought of his own daughter, only a year or two older than Abigail, and imagined her in Abigail's place.

He shook his head, disgusted. "It's enough to make my blood boil, seeing a girl in this state."

"My father used to say that . . . " she muttered.

He paused in brushing out her hair. "I'm sorry?"

"It's nothing."

Strange. Well, there's no point in pressing her, he decided, *not when she's like this.*

"Can you tell me what happened?" he asked. "They asked me to find out for them."

She sighed. "I suppose it all started when my parents told me that he wasn't real. He didn't like that, not at all. Or, perhaps when my parents forced me to take pills that made me never dream."

He frowned, picking out a leaf from her hair. "Pills? You're awfully young for that. Have you been to a psychiatrist before? There's nothing in your medical records . . . "

She shook her head. "Oh no. I've never been to a doctor before. My mother didn't like them. These were something the neighbor cooked up. My mother asked her for something that would make me sleep without dreaming, and the pills did work. For a time." She stared up at the ceiling. "She told me he would drive me mad, and I suppose he has."

"Who is this 'he' you speak of?" he asked, moving onto a new segment of her hair.

"Oh, I can't tell you that. His name is always changing, you see." She looked back at her bare, dirty feet and shifted them slightly. "He was always so kind to me. I'd hate for him to be angry again."

"Has 'he' been angry with you before?"

She laughed, a bitter sound. "Oh no, not with me. With my parents. For making me sleep without dreaming. The people here aren't like that. The people here listened to the neighbor when she said to leave me be. That it's inevitable. That he takes what he wants, and what he wants is me."

He wasn't sure what to say to that, so he just picked carefully at her hair with the brush. "They said you haven't been sleeping," he told her after a moment of silence had passed.

She shook her head again. "Oh, I don't need to anymore. Can't you hear them? They're so loud."

Hallucinations. She's having auditory hallucinations. It's good they called me in.

He finished working through her hair. There was a half-circle of dirt and debris on the wood floor around her from the brushing. He put the brush back in his bag and regarded her seriously. "Abigail, I want you to try to sleep. Can you do that for me?"

She sighed. "I don't see much point in delaying the inevitable, but I suppose I might. It will give me a chance to speak with him. It's better I do that while you're awake."

She stood slowly and turned, keeping her face and her eyes away from him as she moved over to the bed. She lowered herself into it and closed her eyes. She let out a long, slow breath and then started to snore softly. As soon as she was asleep, he sighed with relief. Maybe in the morning, he could try to get some sense out of her.

The next morning, he walked into her room to find her sitting in a different corner, still facing the wall. She seemed to have showered, he noticed. He decided he would have to thank the nurses on the way out for getting her to a bathing facility. She was smiling a little at something she held in her hands. He moved closer and saw it was a small, blue flower.

"Good morning, Doctor Jasper," she said in a conversational tone to the tiny floret in her hands. "How were your dreams?"

"Pleasant," he told her smoothly, sitting down beside her.

She laughed a little. "Liar."

He hesitated. It was true, his dreams had been unsettling, in that amorphous way that dreams sometimes are. He couldn't remember anything clearly, only that there had been something very disturbing about them. He had woken in a cold sweat just before dawn and hadn't been able to get back to sleep.

She continued, "Oh, I spared you some of his wrath, but you still touched my hair. He was angry! Oh, not with me. No, he was very glad to see me. . . but we must stay apart for a little. Just for a little . . . "

She stroked the delicate blue flower.

"Where did you get that?" he asked, trying to ignore her prattle.

She smiled fondly at the blossom in her hands. "He gave it to me." She raised it to her nose to smell, and then blew on it and it was gone, dissolving in her hands like dust. She sighed. "They never last very long here."

"Abigail . . . " he began, putting aside the matter of the disappearing flower. "Do you remember what happened last week, before you were brought here?"

"Of course." She hung her head, staring down at her clean, bare feet. "He was so angry, you see. But I apologize, I shouldn't speak of that . . . "

"You can tell me."

"Can I?" she mused. "When I talked to him, he said you might hurt me. Are you going to try to hurt me, doctor? I would not, if I were you."

"Of course not." Frustrated, he touched her shoulder, hoping she would face him. "I'd like to protect you, to *help* you."

She didn't so much as glance at him. She only laughed again, bitterly this time. "My father—my *parents* were only trying to protect me, to help me, in their own way. It did not save them from his wrath."

"What did he do to them?" he asked, struggling not to lose patience with her. "What did he do to *you*, Abigail?"

She finally moved as if to look at him but stopped abruptly halfway. She twisted away again, back towards the corner. "He has only ever helped me. He saved me."

He frowned. "Saved you? What did you need saving from?"

"I think you had better leave now," she told him. "The longer you are here, the less safe you are. That's what the neighbor told the nurses."

This was new information.

"Why am I not safe? Are you going to attack me?" he asked, half-joking.

She didn't laugh, didn't even smile.

"Please," she whispered. "Go."

He sighed. "Very well. But tomorrow you must tell me what happened to your parents. Are you going to sleep tonight?"

She shook her head. "No. I told you yesterday, didn't I? I don't need to anymore."

"You need to rest, Abigail."

When she didn't respond he touched her shoulder again, trying to get her to look at him. "Please, will you at least try? For me?"

"If it will get you to go, I will promise to sleep. You're not safe here, doctor," she told the wall.

He stood. "I suppose that will have to do. I will leave, then."

He walked to the door and paused, glancing back at her. She still sat curled in her corner, not looking at him. "I'll see you tomorrow, Abigail."

"You shouldn't," she muttered as he opened the door.

He almost turned back to ask her what she meant, but shook his head and left the room. He had other things to do besides unravel her ravings and riddles.

He had other patients. The police could wait. With her mind as fragile as it seemed, he didn't want to press her too hard or too fast. Something was broken within her. There was no point in breaking her further.

He spotted a nurse and flagged her down.

"Do you know who is responsible for Miss Baker today?"

She nodded. "Of course. It's me now, at least until the night shift comes in, and it was Jackie Frazier last night. Why?"

"I wanted to thank whoever made sure Abigail made it to a bathing room. Was that you or Miss Frazier?"

She froze, going pale, her professional smile falling away. "Doctor Jasper . . . none of the nurses have been in her room except to bring her food. That woman, Miss Baker's neighbor, warned us away. We didn't listen, not at first, but . . . well. We've reason to believe she was telling the truth."

He raised an eyebrow at her, confused. "I'm afraid I don't understand. The truth about what? And how did Miss Baker get clean if none of you helped her?"

The nurse only shook her head. "I have my suspicions, doctor, and I expect you'll find out on your own if you keep trying to talk to her. But I would be careful around Miss Baker if I were you. Don't you try to hurt her. Whatever happened to her parents is . . . it's tragic, I'm sure, but it's not worth the price you'll pay."

And then, before he could ask her what she meant, she hurried away from him.

He frowned after her. He was certainly unnerved at times by Abigail, but he didn't think there was anything about her that warranted the kind of fear the nurse had been exhibiting. The more he learned about the girl, the more questions he had. Some part of him wanted to listen to the nurse, to leave her alone. Some inner voice was whispering that he was out of his depth. It had something to do with his restless sleep the night before.

But he was a doctor, a man of science. A few uneasy dreams were no excuse for not doing his job. And his job, at least where Abigail was concerned, was to help her. If in helping her he could find out what happened to her parents, the police would be happy too. However, his primary concern was aiding her in regaining her mind. He would do whatever was necessary.

He woke that night in a cold sweat. He chased after the dream for a moment, trying to remember it and what had disturbed him about it, but it evaded him. All he could recall was an afterimage of a half-familiar green lit hallway. His heart was racing, and he was sick with adrenaline. He looked over at his still-sleeping wife before crawling out of bed. He went into the bathroom and sat on the edge of the bathtub, thinking.

It wasn't like him to have nightmares, even ones he couldn't remember, especially not two nights in a row. There was something about it that was nagging at him. It had something to do with Abigail, but he couldn't think. He was too tired . . . Was it something she had said? Why? She hadn't done anything but stare at the wall in the two days that he'd known her.

She unnerved him. She frightened the nurses. The police

wanted him to try to get her statement, but they hadn't given him a timeline to do so. They were hushing up the story in the press. There was no one rushing him yet. At the same time, he felt he was running out of time. But what could he do to help her? Something in her mind was broken. That would not mend quickly, if at all.

He watched as the darkness in the bathroom window gradually brightened with the coming of dawn. He stood and leaned against the sink, staring at his drawn face in the mirror. He looked tired. He felt tired. Two nights of uneasy dreams was enough to make him think of canceling everything and going back to bed, but he decided against it. He felt like if he tried to go back to sleep, he would only have more nightmares.

Instead, full of a strange vigor, he got dressed and made himself a large pot of coffee. He went out and got the paper, thinking it was a nice morning. Then he sat in the kitchen, steadily drinking his way through the coffee and reading the sports page, until he heard his wife and daughter getting up. His wife made them eggs and toast. He finished his breakfast and went out to the car.

He was tapping his fingers in time with the radio as he drove, still full of that restless energy that had driven him away from going back to sleep. He pulled into the hospital's parking lot and parked in his usual spot. He strode over to the building, and into the psychiatric ward. He showed the guard there his badge and stepped into the section where the criminally insane were kept.

He did his morning rounds, only half paying attention to the ravings of his scheduled patients. After lunch he decided to try talking to Abigail again. He knocked on her door, expecting no answer, and was reaching for the handle when the door began to open. He found a strange woman standing on the other side, blinking at him. She seemed as surprised by him as he felt looking at her.

"You'd be Doctor Jasper, then," she reasoned after a moment, moving to step into the hall. He stepped aside to give her room.

"Yes, Miss . . . ?" he asked.

She stuck out a hand for him to shake. "Sandra Gray. Call me Sandra, please. I'm Abigail's neighbor. I was checking on her."

He took her hand, and then what she'd said registered with him. "Her neighbor? Not the one who made the . . . " He paused, trying to think of the best thing to call them. "The sleeping pills?"

She nodded. "Yes, that one. They were chamomile and a few other herbs to help with sleep, nothing that should have harmed anyone. I'm an herbalist, you see." She sighed then glanced away. "If Mrs. Baker had told me who they were for . . . But by the time I knew, it was too late."

Here, maybe, he could get some answers. "Perhaps you

can tell me what happened to them. Miss Baker's parents. The police think she murdered them and hid their bodies, but I have a hard time believing that."

She bit her lip for a moment, then shook her head. "I can say I have my guesses, but I suspect only Abigail knows for certain what took place that night."

He frowned, thinking. "I'm sure you're right. If I may ask, Miss Gray, why did you warn the nurses to stay away from Miss Baker?"

"Please, call me Sandra." She paused and studied him carefully, head to foot as though examining him, the line of her lips getting thinner as she did. Finally, she shook her head. "Doctor, you should know why I warned them away. The same thing that's happening to you happened to me when I made those pills for Mrs. Baker. *Something to keep dreams away* she said, and I made them. Abigail tells me he wasn't too happy. I've tried to make it right by keeping others from suffering the same fate."

"Who is this 'he'? Miss Baker keeps—" He broke off, seeing someone he knew walking their way. "Officer McCall."

"Doctor Jasper," Officer McCall acknowledged. "I was just coming to ask you if you'd had any luck with Abigail Baker. The Captain wants this put to bed as soon as possible."

He shook his head. "It's not that she's uncooperative, but . . . "

"She's not all there, eh?" Officer McCall asked knowingly. "Well, I can't say I'm surprised. Do what you can, hmm?"

Sandra scowled at the officer before looking back to the doctor. "I'm sure she's told you more than she dares, doctor. You're like Icarus, with his wings of wax, and Abigail is the sun. From the look of you, you're too close already."

"Are you implying I'm in danger from Miss Baker?" he asked, raising an eyebrow at her.

"Not exactly."

"Oh, she doesn't know what she's talking about," Officer McCall interjected. "I took her statement when we picked up Miss Baker. It was so useful; the Captain tossed the entire thing in the waste bin."

Sandra flushed. "I hadn't been sleeping well. I'd be happy to give the statement again."

Officer McCall snorted. "There's no point. It's like I told the good doctor here, the Captain wants this whole thing done with."

Something she'd said had caught the doctor's attention.

"You mentioned that you hadn't been sleeping well when you gave your statement. Why not?" he asked.

She raised an eyebrow at him. "You tell me. Why do you seem so tired today?"

"It's nothing," he lied. "I'm a doctor, we're always tired. It's something we learn to live with while we're still learning."

"Leave the man alone with your nonsense," Officer McCall ordered. "You probably shouldn't be here. Maybe I should give orders that you're not to be allowed in."

Sandra shook her head. "I'll go. I know when I'm not wanted. But listen here, Doctor Jasper." She leaned in close to him. "You seem smart and nice enough, so I'll give you the same warning I gave the nurses. Stay away from Abigail, if you can. Don't dare try to harm her. If you do not heed me, you will regret it."

With that she turned and walked away, every inch of her reading annoyance. He shook his head as he watched her go. He wondered why everyone seemed to think he was going to attempt to hurt Abigail. He knew he would never harm a patient, particularly not one as fragile as she was.

"Ah, do you want me to go and collect Miss Gray there?" Officer McCall asked. "Technically that counted as a threat."

He shook his head. "No, I'm fine." He laid his hand on the door handle to Abigail's room, and grinned. "Besides, she's only a woman. What's she going to do?"

"Ha. Right."

"Good afternoon, Doctor Jasper," Abigail's voice greeted him when he walked into the room. "How were your dreams?"

He peered around the room, searching for her. He closed

the door and found, to his annoyance, that not only was she in a different corner, again, but she was hiding behind the door.

"Are you going to start with that now too?" he asked, irritated. She shrugged, and he sighed. "I'm sorry. I met your neighbor outside — frustrating woman — but I shouldn't take it out on you. How are you today? Did you sleep?"

She didn't respond for a moment. "I slept," she answered at last. "Doctor, I must warn you, he does not like you. He says you are going to try to hurt me. I feel I should ask you to leave, for both of our sakes."

"Abigail, you must have realized by now that I can't just keep leaving. I want to help you, and to do that I need to talk to you." He knelt next to her on the floor. "Now, will you tell me what happened to your parents?"

She hesitated again, and then let out a long, slow sigh. "They heard your conversation in the hallway, after Sandra left. I really must ask you to leave, doctor. You're not safe here. I no longer believe you mean me no harm."

He throttled down his rising anger and put his hand on her shoulder, trying to make her face him. "I regret that you overheard what I said about Miss Gray, Abigail. I didn't mean it, not really. Listen, I'll apologize to her next time she's here. You're safe with me, you are."

She shook her head. "I'm sorry, Doctor Jasper, but you had

better leave. He won't show you any more mercy. And I will not ask it of him again."

He felt the already stretched thin strand of his patience with her begin to fray. He picked her up out of the corner and sat her on the bed. He stood in front of her, leaning towards her, while she stared at the floor.

"Abigail Baker," he scolded, his voice rising, "you are not in danger from me! But you *are* in danger from the police! They think you killed your parents and hid their bodies! I need you to tell me what happened that night, or they'll keep you here for the rest of your natural life! Do you understand me?"

"My father hit me," she said quietly.

"What?"

"My father hit me," she repeated. "And they told him, and he came. He was so angry that he threw my parents into a nightmare."

Finally, he was getting somewhere. "Which they? And who is 'he'?"

"I've told you, his name is always changing." She sighed then. "When I was small, before I learned to know his name, I called him the King of Dreams."

A drug dealer maybe? he wondered. "Where can I find him? Are your parents still alive?"

She shrugged. "My parents were alive last I knew. And he

is coming. One of them left to fetch him. They are worried for me now. They do not trust you."

Her parents were *alive*! Maybe, he hoped, he could find out where they were. "Abigail, listen, focus. I need to know where your parents are."

"I've told you where they are."

His patience, beyond frayed now, finally snapped. "You've told me nothing, you worthless girl!" he roared, and swung back a hand to slap her.

An unknown hand caught his on the back swing, and he found himself flung hard into the corner where Abigail had been sitting when he entered the room. He struggled to his feet, looking around frantically for his attacker. He saw no one in the room besides Abigail, only a dark shadow in the shape of a man before him.

She moved to stand beside the dark figure, staring at him. Her wide eyes were an unnatural, electric green. Something about them reminded him of his uneasy dreams the night before. He wanted to turn and run from the room, but he couldn't move, pinned like an insect on a cork board by the intensity of her gaze. He could barely breathe.

There was a deep rumbling, a voice speaking words in a language he could not understand. Abigail shook her head, and spoke in the same rasping language to the shadowy figure. All the while, her wide green eyes had him pinned. After a moment more of shared speech in that unearthly tongue, the shadow faded from view, and the doctor and Abigail were alone. The light in her eyes went out, and he found he could move again.

"What?" he asked, panting.

She sighed, laying her hand on the side of her face where he would have slapped her. "I tried to warn you. They tell me the nurse and Sandra did as well. Do not attempt to hurt me." She walked to the door and opened it. "You had better go now, doctor. Go home. You're tired, and not thinking clearly. It will only be worse from now on."

"But—"

She shook her head. "Go."

He hesitated for a moment longer before leaving the room, feeling dazed. He checked out of the hospital. He drove home. He watched the television and ate an early dinner. He laid down in his bed, still fully dressed, and closed his eyes. He felt himself drift off to sleep.

And then the nightmare truly began.

Three Times True

Three times true as the old ones say
Three times said as the light dies away
Hopes and dreams come here to die
As I sing my lullaby

Let me sing you a spell
Is this heaven or hell?

Three times true as the old ones say
Three times done by the light of day
Fickle friends, a suspicious mind
Do not seek, you will always find

Let me sing you a spell
Is this heaven or hell?

Three time true as the old ones say
I did not speak, I just went away
I sang songs on the hanging tree
As they tied that noose on me

Let me sing you a spell
Where is heaven or hell?

Hopes and dream come here to die
As I sing my lullaby
I'm still at the hanging tree
Can anybody hear me?

About June

I didn't write much in June
I didn't have much to say
I was just trying to listen
My silent world went away

For a month now the world has been screaming
For a month I did nothing but hear
To those who know more than I can ever
To the words of those living in fear

There's so much that I am still learning
There's so much that I do not know
The truth of it is this world is hurting
The truth is we all need to grow

I hope that someday we do better
That everyone stands side by side
Not longer screaming, but learning
Together we must turn the tide

If you are still screaming back, listen!
If you are still listening, great!
We all need to hear now the silence
That those who are missing create

Hindsight

Whose voices have you not been hearing?
Whose voices have been forced to leave?
Whose voices should really be raised now?
Whose voices should we most receive?

It's not my voice that we need to hear now
My voice speaks with privilege, it lies
And so now I step back to listen again
So others, who know more, can rise

Weather the Storm

I don't really know what to tell you
I'm not really sure what to say
I have hardly spoken to someone
I do not live with today

My words have run out like the sand
From an hourglass turned upside down
It's all topsy turvy, a little bit curvy
We're all trying not to drown

Someday the world will turn over
And all will be righted once more
Until then I urge you, whoever
To stay home and weather the storm

Sturgeon Moon

The Children of the Sky

The Elders always told me that catching a falling star would burn me, but I tried it all the same. She fell into my hands, so small and beautiful and bright, still shining. Small enough to fit in my pocket almost. Small enough that she needed to be cradled and cuddled. She was crying. She was only a baby.

I wrapped her up in my cloak and took her home. What else could I do with her? Leave her out for the void beasts to find? Never. And she hadn't burned me, after all. I gave her some goats milk, and she drank it, chortling happily at me when she was done. I sat with her in my little house, just looking at her, and tried to decide what to do.

"I suppose I should name you," I told her as she tried to

chew on her foot. I reached out and touched one of her sheer white curls. "How about Astara?" She giggled and smiled toothlessly up at me. I took this as a good sign. "Astara, then."

She grew rapidly, in that way that babies do. I swear I blinked, and she was walking, but months had gone by without my noticing. One day follows another so quickly once you have a child to raise. She was a sweet, happy baby. I wanted to hide her, but I knew it was impossible. After she had started to walk, I took her to the Elders.

Miga, the Eldest, watched my adopted daughter wobble around. "What is this?" he asked me.

"My daughter Astara," I answered evenly.

"You have no lover, no wife," Alise, the Matron, observed.

"No, but I have a daughter."

Astara toddled over to Miga and grinned up at him, drooling.

Miga sighed. "She is a fallen star. Anyone can see that." He looked down at Astara's shining face, and his stern demeanor cracked. He smiled back at her. "But anyone can see you are unharmed, and she is a sweet child. I vote she may stay, for now."

"For now," agreed Alise. And so, it went around the room. My daughter could stay, if only temporarily.

When Astara was three, and fast asleep in her bed, I again went walking at night in the deep forest meadows not far from my home. I saw a piece of sky fall, and I caught it in my hands. This time it was a baby boy. Dark, as Astara was light. I wrapped him in my cloak and took him home. I gave him goats milk, named him Claec.

Astara was thrilled to meet her new baby brother. Claec was fascinated by her. He crawled after her as soon as he was able. He loved looking up at his fair sister with his wide eyes, dark like the night sky. I took him to the Elders sooner than I had with Astara. He was only a few days old. They looked troubled but agreed that Claec could stay as well.

My third child, Xefiev, fell from the sky in a gust of wind. The winds blew wild around the village, and the Elders issued an ultimatum. The children would have to go. I had an ultimatum of my own. I would go with them. The Elders agreed. They gave us some food and supplies. Off we went, into the blasted lands where the void beasts roamed.

"It will be alright, children," I told the six-year-old Astara and three-year-old Claec, with little Xefiev sleeping soundly on my back. "We will find our own place, and all will be well."

"Yes, father," Astara agreed brightly.

"All be well," Claec said with a grin.

The wind tousled my hair as I walked on through the blasted lands.

That night I built a fire on the barren land. I first fed the goat and the mule I had been allowed to bring with me, and then the children. I found I was not hungry, only exhausted and heartsick.

"Father, eat!" Astara pushed some of her food at me.

"Eat!" Claec agreed.

"Perhaps in the morning," I told them. Shortly after, we all laid down to sleep.

I woke in the middle of the night to the soft voices of the children. We were surrounded by void beasts, and I knew we were doomed. The void beasts would destroy us, as they destroyed all things. I grabbed Xefiev and Astara and pulled them under me, hoping to protect them. Claec had already wandered towards the void beasts, out of my reach.

"Claec, come here!" I wailed.

He ignored me and went closer to the void beasts. The one nearest to him let out a shrieking hiss. Its voice was like knives in my ears, and I heard Astara and Xefiev cry under me.

Claec, seemingly unafraid, waved a hand in front of his face. "Stinky!" he complained.

Then he screamed back at the void beast, and he did so with a voice like thunder that growled up from the depths of the earth all the way to the sky. The void beasts fled into the night. I climbed off Astara and Xefiev, cradling them both until they stopped crying. Claec walked back over.

"All be well," he told me with a smile.

I nodded and pulled him into the hug with Astara and Xefiev.

We moved on. Eventually, we came to a forest, past the blasted lands, and there we made our new home.

Xefiev grew up to be trouble, full of mischief. He delighted in teasing Astara and Claec. He would listen to me, when it suited him to do so. I was never sure what to do, or what to tell him, to make him behave. Surely a day would come that his mischief would cause him trouble.

More children fell from the sky to land in my arms. Dionmachus, Akylen, Suitar, and Bobris, to name a few. Some fell at night; some fell during the day. I came to expect it almost any given year, when the oldest were old enough to help me care for the youngest.

I did not age. This troubled me. But as years went on and the children grew, I noticed most of them did not age past twenty or so. I thought perhaps it was the place we had found. Something in the forest, in the earth and air.

All of the children developed little quirks. Astara still glittered and shone, just like the star she had been. Claec was dark, and the few times we were threatened by void beasts, he chased them away with ease. Xefiev controlled the wind when he was older.

The children, most of them, wandered off into the world as they grew, as children do, but always they would wander back. Except for Dionmachus, who stayed with me in the house I had built for the children.

"I do not wish to leave the forest," he told me when I asked. "The forest is my home. But you, father, you should go and see the world. Aren't you curious?"

"I am content to raise my children," I said with a smile.

"None of us have fallen from the sky for a hundred years," Dionmachus pointed out. "I think the sky has given up all of her children for you to raise."

He was not wrong. This had weighed on me and depressed me for many years. At the same time, in many ways, it was a relief. After the years of chaos, raising my adopted brood, there was peace in the silence. But it was a lonely peace. Dionmachus was right. I missed my children.

And so back out into the wide world I went. When I left the forest, I found a vast plain where, once, there had only been the blasted lands. Rolling waves of golden grass rippled in a gentle breeze. I stared at it for a long time, remembering the days when only void beasts had roamed those lands, and wondered what else had changed during my time in the forest.

Akylen found me that evening and walked with me through the plains for several days after. We talked of many things, the grasses, where to find water and food, how to hunt. Akylen was a great hunter and caught most of the game as we traveled.

At length, an encampment of tents appeared on the horizon. "There are my people, the Kylen," Akylen told me with a proud smile. "They have adopted me as a god. I do what I can to protect and guide them."

"A god?" I asked, frowning, but he did not answer. We went to the encampment together.

The Kylen were happy to see Akylen. I could see they were curious about me as well, although they were too polite to ask what they wanted to know. All but one, a small child of perhaps four or five.

The child clutched at my leg, grinning. "What are you the god of?" they asked with a cheerful, guileless grin. A woman, the child's mother, pulled them away a moment later, but the question remained with me.

I left the Kylen, and Akylen told me to head south for the coast. I met my son Suitar there, who took me in a boat across the sea. He taught me to sail, and I asked him if he also had people who called him a god, as with his brother Akylen.

He nodded. "All sailors hail me as their god, and I favor them with good wind and fair weather when I can."

"But you are not a god," I tried to object. My children? Gods?

He only laughed, a hearty chuckle. "Father, you caught us out of the sky. What did you think we were?"

For this, I had no answer.

Suitar took me to the great trade city of Jun, where they grew and sold a great many spices. Here I found my daughter Astara, sitting in a temple with no roof so that there was an open view of the sky and sun and stars. She embraced me and called me 'father' and the people gathered nearby began to whisper.

And so, I went from city to town to clan, visiting my children, who called me 'father'. Often, I was accompanied by Suitar while I was at sea. Bobris came with me while I was on foot, following the road. My children's people called me 'Father of the Gods' and asked my name. I realized I no longer remembered it. I had only been 'father' to my children for many hundreds of years.

Eventually, I stopped seeking my children and went high into the mountains to think. Here there was snow, and thick, dense trees. And no one to call me father. I wanted to think, to understand. How had this happened?

I climbed higher, past the trees and snow, and although I could feel the cold, I did not mind it. I still had not aged, and this troubled me. What had I become? I had been born a mortal man. What was I now? Who was I now? The Father of the Gods?

"Why me?" I asked the clear blue sky when I reached the top of the mountain. "Why did you give Astara, and Claec, and

Xefiev, and all of the others to me? I am — I was — just a man!"

There was no answer from the sky. There had never been any answers from the sky, only children for me to love and raise. I waited there for a very long time. I watched the stars come out and asked again. I asked again at dawn, and once more at sunset. The next day, I asked over and over again, the whole day long. How many times I asked, how many days went by, I do not know. I cannot say.

There was never any answer from the sky.

At last, I walked down the mountain into the snow. A few flakes drifted gently around me, and I reached out my hand and caught one. In my hands, I held a tiny baby with white hair and piercing blue eyes. I wrapped him carefully in my cloak as he began to fuss and decided this was my answer.

Maybe I was just a man, just a father. Maybe the sky would give me no answer in words, but she would give me children to love. I was the man who had caught a falling star, and a piece of sky, and a breath of wind, and so many others. Perhaps I was more than a normal man after all. I was the Father of the Gods of Beyle.

I climbed down the mountain and brought my new son home.

Heartstring

There's so many things I want to tell you
I agree with so much of what's been said
I also feel like I'm drowning
In the pool of my mind and my head

Sometimes we need intermissions
And the universe, it coldly says "No"
We're forced to move forward, hearts aching
Into darkness where we don't want to go

But sometimes there is a reprieve
And sometimes that hurts even worse
We feel the pain we were ignoring
In the pause between each starting verse

Remember if you can in this feeling
The pain and the healing it brings
There's so much that we've been ignoring
In this new silence, everyone sings

We're all learning that we are broken
And learning to mend where we may
If we all work together I think we might find
The pieces we've all thrown away

Here is a piece of my heartstring
Can you lend me an ear for this rhyme?
I wish now that I could hold you
And tell you that everything's fine

Hindsight

We all know that I would be lying
We know now we're falling apart
But tomorrow, next week, next year maybe
We'll all learn to make a new start

My hope for the darkness and silence
That covers the world as I write
Is that we're all healing and mending
And soon we'll be bathing in light

Gods and Angels

All the gods and angels, are you listening to me?
I have never been the best follower, you see
I barely believe in what I can see and touch
So I don't believe in gods and angels that much

Personal disaster brings out the worst in me
I don't like who I am, I don't like who I'll be
Reaching out for help that I have not earned at all
I'm trying to fly when I know that I should fall

If any gods are listening, I don't know what to say
I know what I am losing; I wish it was okay
I don't really pray and I do not like to ask
For what I know is an impossible task

So instead I'm asking for strength I know I've got
Help me find it now, I'm not asking a lot
All the gods and angels that I do not believe in
Forgive me for this weakness, forgive me for this sin

All the gods and angels, are you listening to me?
It sometimes feels like I'm alone, adrift and lost at sea
The sea is grief and pain, and I know I'm not okay
So thank you all for listening to my song today

All my friends and family, please reach out a hand
Lead me from this darkness, lend me the strength to stand
More than gods and angels, I am now looking to you
To find my way in darkness, to show me what to do

In The Dark

It's dark in the car
Too dark to see the keyboard
But I keep typing
Because that's what I am
I'm writing
That's all that I am
That's all that I've been
Words on paper
Words in my head
And I wonder
Is that how I reach you?
Words on paper
That fell out of my head?
I've wondered forever
If I write you a letter
Would you read it?
If I put myself on paper
Like I always have
Will you see me?
Will you understand?
It must be so hard
Being part of the world
But always a little outside
She saw you
I want you to know
I see you too
Although
I cannot see
My keyboard
In the dark of the car

Corn Moon

The Bargain

Ushina swept her Master's study dutifully. Master Hikaru was kind, but she obviously was not very good about cleaning. She sneezed – again – and went over to the window to open it and let out the dust. As she leaned over the ancient bookcase and opened the window, she knocked down one of the scrolls. It fell to the floor and rolled open.

"Oh no . . . " she groaned. She began to roll it closed again, and then paused, seeing the signature at the bottom of the scroll.

Xefiev.

The Mad God had written something? She glanced at the doorway, listening for her Master. From the sound of the snores down the hallway, Master Hikaru was taking a nap. Surely she had time? She looked closer at the scroll. The writing was difficult to make out, but she thought she could read it.

> I never meant what I have done. It was a joke, a jest between brothers. Or so I thought at the time. But now, Lrias will not forgive me, and I do not deserve his forgiveness. My other brothers and my sisters have sentenced me, and I will carry out that sentence. Five hundred years I will sit alone in my prison.
>
> I will kill any who dare disturb me before my time is up. It will grieve me, but it must be done. That is the Bargain I have made. This is the only warning I can give you. Stay away from my prison. It is not worth the price you will pay to seek me out. Even after my sentence is up, I wish to be left alone.
>
> Mother Sky, I pray that my people will not suffer too much for what I have done.
>
> *Xefiev*

Ushina carefully rolled up the scroll when she reached the end, taking care with the old parchment. She would have to ask Master Hikaru about this later. What did the Mad God mean about

Lrias? No one had seen Lrias in . . . well, since before the war started, probably. She stood to turn around, scroll in hand, and heard a rattle behind her.

She whirled in time to see an arm pulling back from the window, a scroll in hand.

"Thief!" she snarled, and vaulted out the open window. She landed lightly on the roof under the window and scanned the street below. There. She leapt off the roof and sprinted after the man running swiftly away from her Master's house.

"Stop! Thief!" she yelled, hoping someone would stop the strange man, but the streets were empty. It was just the thief and her. He turned a corner, and she lunged around it, her feet skidding as she tried to turn without slowing down.

Sprinting was not her specialty. She was a distance runner, slow, steady, and methodical. The thief she chased was faster than she was, but not by much. Still, he was gaining ground ahead of her.

"Wind, aid me," she panted as she ran, and the wind around her picked up. She felt a little stronger for it and quickened her steps. The thief turned another corner, and she smiled. He would be trapped. That was a dead end street. She skidded around the corner, and saw he was still running.

He was running straight for a building she knew, and she was filled with a sharp stab of terrified horror. Did he not know what it was?

"Stop, you fool!" she called after him. "That's Xefiev's Cage!" He kept running full tilt towards it. "You'll be killed!"

She put in an extra spurt of energy and sprinted with all her might towards him, almost catching him as he opened the door. She skidded to a halt before the building, watching, horrified, as he stepped inside. He fell the moment he crossed the threshold. She saw a red vapor rise from him before he dissolved into dust. The wind behind her pressed her closer to the doorway, scattering the man shaped pile of dust in the doorway.

Hesitantly she took the last two steps towards the building and moved to close the door. She stopped with her hand on the door handle as someone reached out of Xefiev's Cage, holding the scroll. She stared at the bone white hand, and reached out with trembling fingers to take the scroll. She started again to close the door, and froze when a voice spoke from within.

"Ushina," the voice said.

The Mad God knew her name? How?

"Yes, Xefiev?" she asked with a voice she could not recognize.

"Stay," the voice said. "Do not enter, but tell me; how fare my people?"

She stood mute before the doorway. Where would she even begin?

"Look at me," the voice ordered. When she only stared at the door handle under her trembling fingers, the hand came out again, and lifted her chin.

Bright hair, like flame, danced in the mischievous wind. That same mischief danced in kind blue eyes. A young face, not much older than hers, a smile teasing at his lips. Those lips parted and she heard again the voice of Xefiev, the Mad God, speaking to her.

"Do not fear me, Ushina," he told her, "for you have nothing to fear so long as you stay outside the walls of my prison. Tell me truthfully. How do my people fare?"

She blinked and bit her lip, avoiding his gaze. "I'm not sure where to start . . . What do you know?"

"Assume I know nothing. It has been five hundred twenty seven years, two hundred forty five days, and six hours since I last spoke to one of my people. It has been sixteen years since anyone dared to enter my prison, even. Tell me. How fare my people?"

He released her and she let out a breath she didn't know she'd been holding. She looked back down at the door handle, trying to gather her thoughts. Assume he knew nothing? How could she possibly sum up over five hundred years of history, some of which she did not even know?

Almost audible in her ears was the voice of Master Jian, the eldest Master. *"Start with what you know, daft child."*

She bowed slightly to Xefiev before speaking. "We are still at war with the Lrian. There is a famine this year — the Lrian burned many of our farms — and the Masters are wondering how we are to feed ourselves. There are twenty Masters, the only elders in the tribe. This is our last settlement. Many of the children are orphans."

She stated each fact as though reciting her lessons, staring at her feet. When she finished there was a silence.

"And tell me . . . what do my people think of me?" Xefiev asked.

"You . . . " She grimaced, but continued, still staring at her feet. "You are called the Mad God. I do not think many people remember you. They remember your cage as a place to avoid. The caretakers — sometimes they made me mind them by threatening to bring me here."

"I see." His voice was quiet.

She bowed again. "Forgive me for bearing you ill news, god of the winds."

"And you, Ushina? What do you think of me?" The question caught her off guard, and she looked up at the Mad God again, startled. He gave her what was probably supposed to be a reassuring smile. "Do not fear. Tell me the truth."

She straightened. What did she think of Xefiev, the Mad God? She opened her mouth, thinking of the scroll she had found, and then closed it again. She remembered the summer breezes murmuring in her ears. The way the winter gales would freeze her friends to the bone, but never her. The way, just moments ago, she had called upon the wind for strength. Hadn't that strength been given? The way the winds, even now, seemed to be almost embracing her. But that scroll . . .

Do not fear, he had said. Very well.

She stood straight, looked him in the eye, and spread her feet apart. She placed her hands on her hips. "I think you are a coward."

He blinked at her. "I beg your pardon?"

"You're a coward!" The words burst from her. "Everyone knows you started the war somehow! So you were imprisoned by the other gods . . . but you've been able to leave your cage for over twenty years! You could have stopped the war before I was even born! My parents might be alive! By the skies above, what is wrong with you?"

Unthinking, she took a step towards him, crossing the threshold of the building.

"All you care about is yourself!" she continued, taking another step, and shoved him. "All the old tales say so! You only ever cared about *your* happiness, about your *clever tricks*! What about your *people*? You are a selfish coward, Xefiev, and you have doomed our tribe to ruin and death! That is what I think of you!

Coward!"

She glared at him when she was done. He rubbed at his chest where she had shoved him, and stared at her. Then, to her surprise, he grinned, a reckless smile of wild glee.

"Ushina. You're standing in my cage," he told her, and she heard the door close behind her.

"No . . . " She spun and tried the door, but it wouldn't open. "No! Xefiev, please! Let me out!" She jiggled the handle, but it wouldn't turn. She faced him again, pressing herself against the door and staring at him as he advanced slowly towards her.

"So," he said, placing a hand on the door on either side of her head. "It seems, young Ushina, that you are trapped in here with the Mad God. What shall we do? What shall we do?" He tucked a lock of her hair behind her ear, and she flinched.

"Don't play with me like a cat with a mouse," she snapped. "If you're going to kill me, do it quickly."

"Now, where is the fun in that?" he asked, his voice playful. "Especially when there is a Bargain to be made?"

She stared up at him, at his mad smile. "A Bargain? What Bargain?"

"Why, a Bargain for your life, of course."

"What about a Bargain for the life of our tribe?" she asked, thinking fast, and had the pleasure of seeing Xefiev's smile fade a little. "Our tribe is dying, Xefiev. We're going to lose the war. Stop the war, or help us win, and I will make any Bargain you ask of me."

He pushed away from her and walked away into the bare cell. The winds outside rattled the door as he paced restlessly, and she tried to open it again. It didn't work. At last he stopped and stared at her, his blue eyes glowing unnaturally in the dim cell. She felt a shiver run down her spine.

"There is a Bargain," he told her. "You will not like it."

"Tell me."

"I will stop the war, as I am responsible for its inception. It will take time. But you, Ushina . . . you must fight beside me in this war. That is the price you must pay. And there is still a toll to pay to keep your life." He stepped closer to her, fingering her cheek.

She ignored the quaking in her stomach and slapped his hand away. "I am not afraid to fight in the war," she lied. "What of this toll?"

He smiled and leaned in very close to her. She resisted the urge to pull away, telling herself firmly that she was not afraid of him. "Something so simple, but so very difficult, Ushina. I wonder if you can pay it?" He leaned in a little closer, the glowing blue light from his eyes spilling onto her face.

"Spit it out, Xefiev. Stop dancing around it and tell me this toll." She reached out to shove him away.

He moved away and caught her hand. He held it, his grip

gentle but firm. "A kiss, Ushina. One for each day you live. If you fail to pay this toll, I shall be forced to kill you." He tugged her arm up, forcing her to take a step closer to him. His free arm snaked around her, pulling her flush against him. "I would hate to kill you, Ushina."

"Why a kiss?" she demanded, struggling to free herself from his grasp.

"Because the winds like you." The answer took her by surprise, and she blinked. He leaned in close to whisper in her ear, "Tell me, Ushina. Do we have a Bargain?"

She bit her tongue, cursing internally. What choice did she have? Her life, the lives of her tribe, they all depended on this Bargain. He was right, she didn't like it. Not the price or the toll she would need to pay.

"We have a Bargain," she snarled. "Now, let me go and open the door. I must tell the Masters."

"Ah ah ah," he chided. "A Bargain such as this one must be sealed."

And he turned his head and pressed his lips against hers. He moved and she found herself pressed against the doorway. He pressed firmly against her as his mouth moved over hers, robbing her of her sense. She heard the winds outside the door fall still. Finally he pulled back from her a pace, and she reached up and slapped him.

He chuckled. "Shall we make a wager, you and I?"

"No," she snapped and turned to open the door.

"I wager that by the end of the war you will be in love with me."

She froze with her hand on the door. "If I am not?"

"We will dispense with the toll." She felt him lean in close to whisper in her ear. "And *when* you are in love with me . . . you will bear my demigod."

Anything to get out of the toll. She shoved him away with her shoulder as she turned. She spat in her palm and held it out to him. "A wager."

He spat in his palm also and took hers. "A wager I look forward to winning."

She squeezed his hand tighter than was necessary. "In your dreams." She released his hand and wiped her hand on her pants. "And now, I must tell the Masters."

"I will join you." He opened the door for her, and she stepped out into the empty street. Only then did she remember the scroll in her hand. She looked down at it and sighed.

Gods. She was going to be in so much trouble.

Goblin

I am a goblin that's running
While I'm lying asleep in my bed
Creeping and sneaking and laughing
In the dreaming inside of my head

I am the moon and the shadows
I am the shriek in the night
I am the creak in the door frame
I am afraid of the light

The morning light, it will wake me
And I'll be a human once more
No longer the moon and the shadows
No longer the creak in the door

Let me sleep longer and deeper
Let me live deep in my mind
Where I am a goblin that's running
Let me leave daylight behind

Let me feast, let me fight, let me frolic
On mountains, let my ragged clothes blow
Let me gather up trinkets and baubles
Let the goblin inside of me show

Hindsight

The real world is harsh and unfriendly
In the real world, I do not belong
When I am a goblin and dreaming
I am brave, I am wise, I am strong

Tonight I will paint my face gaudy
With blue and green streaks, I'll be free
And nevermore shall the world find it
The human that lives inside of me

The Bridge of Death

Blast the music loud, as loud as it will go
Take my seat and wait; I actually do know
It's not like I imagine it, it's not like it's not true
See the fences on the bridge? It's the best that they could do
Blast the music loud and someone, please, hold my hand
As I travel by bus over the cursed land
I know I will be fine, I know I will not fall
Many cross the bridge, but never is it all
Too many have fallen, have crept over the side
Afraid of their own shadows, of things they cannot hide
I call it the Bridge of Death, and I have seen it's ghosts
I cross it with trepidation, but I'm smarter than most
Most fear the height, and some don't like the chain link
But I know what it's for, for those standing on the brink
So never trust the Bridge of Death to hold you up so high
It will try to trick you into thinking you can fly
Better have the fencing, better to break the bridge
Than to someday find yourself standing on the ledge

Hey Siri

I'm trying to find the answers
For what I'm going through
Hey Siri, can you tell me
What it is that I should do?

Alexa has no answers
Cortana doesn't care
Google redirects me
It doesn't matter where

So hello again Facebook
Time to Twitter out my heart
To word vomit on your pages
As I'm tearing apart

The sun is out and shining
It's gorgeous out today
I should go out and see it
Instead of hide away

But she's gone away and left us
We're left without her light
It's dark, it's cold, it's empty
I'm numb here in the night

Harvest Moon

The Fae Will Take Your Name

"Stay away from Fae circles, child. The Fae will take yer name from ye, and even yer own Ma will not know what te call ye."

That was what her grandfather would tell her as they skirted the edge of a strange circle in the middle of the forest. She remembered this during all her rambling through the woods as a child, even as a teenager, and stayed away from the circle. When she grew up and went to college, she forgot.

It was a hot summer night, towards the end of college, and she was home with her parents. She said something, it just slipped out, and then she was running through the woods with her father's voice still ringing in her ears.

"You're no child of mine!"

Tears prickled at her eyes and branches lashed at her arms as she ran. She realized she was going to break an ankle if she didn't start watching where she was going . . . she slowed to a walk, wiping at her face. Only then did she see she was standing in the middle of the wide circle. Old fear rose in her mouth, and she whirled to go back the way she had come. She yelped and backed up a pace when she found a strange, man-like creature standing behind her.

His hair was green. His skin, under the full moonlight, was the same color as the sky at dusk and patterned with lavender stripes, like a cat. His eyes were a blazing orange color, like fire, and glowed brightly with a strange light.

"Foolish mortal!" the Fae creature intoned. "You have stepped into our circle — now you must pay the toll! Give me your name and trespass here no more!"

She licked her lips, opened her mouth, and then stopped. She hadn't come to this part yet. Frantic, she glanced around the clearing.

"Stalling will do you no good, mortal! Speak!"

"It's, um. Leaf?"

The Fae eyed her suspiciously. "What jest is this?"

She shook her head. "No, you're right, sorry. Stick? That sounds stupid. Okay. Petal? No . . . "

The Fae glowed eerily. "Give me your name, impertinent

mortal, or I will take your very life from you!"

"I haven't got one yet!" She burst into tears and hid her face in her hands. "Listen, I'm trans, okay? I've had a horrible night! I accidentally came out to my parents and they kicked me out and I didn't even know I was here and I have no idea what my name is, so . . . so . . . "

She waited for the crack of doom, for the creature to kill her, but it didn't come. She lifted her face from her hands and looked at him. He was still eerie, still terrifying, but the light in his eyes looked somehow more sympathetic. He smiled with a mouth full of shark teeth, but this smile was almost reassuring.

"Child, I told you to give me your name," the Fae creature said again.

She sighed. "Look, I haven't got one! I—"

"No, girl, listen to me. Give me the name your parents gave you. It will trouble you no more. No more will it follow you. You will be free to pick another one that suits you better, be it Lichen, Moss, or Mushroom."

"Oh."

She spat a name, then, her voice filled with hatred. The Fae creature nodded once and disappeared in a bright flash of green that momentarily blinded her. Quickly, she ran to the edge of the circle and out of it. Then she stopped, remembering her manners, and turned.

"Thank you!" she called into the circle. There was no answer, and she turned and walked slowly back towards her parent's house. She would need to at least go and get her school bag . . . She would need that for the fall semester of school. She could always crash at Kenny's house. He would understand, maybe. . .

She walked into the light of the yard and heard a soft cry. She looked up. Her mother moved from the doorway where she had been waiting and rushed towards her. Her mother took her hands as if to warm them. She felt her eyes fill with tears. Did this mean she wasn't angry?

"Oh! I've been so worried about you!" her mother fussed. "Don't worry about what *that man* said before you ran outside. Hrmph! Please, come inside— oh!" Her mother's eyes went wide. "I can't even recall your . . . what's that term I was just reading? Your deadname? I guess it really never suited you. Don't worry about it, sweetheart. I'll help you pick out something new, something good."

This was too much, and she found herself crying again.

A year later, now a graduate, she was walking through the woods. She was thinking about that summer night, and all that had changed for the better. She found a boy sitting on a rock, looking troubled, and thought she recognized the look on his face. She had worn it often enough.

"Are you lost?" she asked.

The boy looked up, startled.

She smiled, trying to look reassuring. "I'm Acacia. I'm visiting my mom, she's just over the hill. What's your name?"

He frowned, looking almost pained. "Andrew, or, no, I mean, um . . . Craig, maybe?"

She laughed. "I know the feeling. It took me a while to settle on Acacia. Hey, listen . . . there's this place . . . "

She took his hand and drew him through the woods.

Pants

I turned pants into a shirt today
They didn't fit me
So I made them something else
That does fit
I didn't ask for permission
Even though you gave them to me
Kind of like
How I changed my name
I kept the core of what you gave me
I only changed it a little
But now the name fits
Like the pants
That are now a shirt
I'm sorry I didn't ask you
But you would have said no
And I can't give the name back
It's mine now
And so
I turned the name you gave me
Into a name that fits me
I can't undo what I've done
And I don't want to
Just like I can't uncut
The pants
That are more comfortable
As a shirt

Can You Recall

Can you recall
Do you remember at all
A query I made when I was three?
I must have scared you
Because you didn't answer
In a way that satisfied me

I know it must be hard, my being this way
I need an answer to that question today
Writing this poem doesn't fill me with joy
But mommy, when will I be a real boy?

Do you understand?
I'm not a woman or a man
I am something somewhere in the in-between
Neither son nor daughter
I know it's kind of awkward
Not knowing what to call me

I know it must be hard, my being this way
I just want you to call me 'Eli' today
Writing this poem is a dizzy kind of whirl
But mommy, when will I be a real girl?

Hindsight

Do you remember
From that cold December
The words that I wrote down in verse?
You did not acknowledge
The words I had written
And somehow that made everything worse

It's so hard for me, you being this way
I don't know how else to talk to you today
Writing this poem almost fills me with fear
Can't you see mom, I'm genderqueer

Face

I look at my face in the mirror
The zits and the scars
And the lines
The bags under eyes

I try out a smile
But it fades away
Like the sun
Which has gone down

I'm tired of that face
Give me a new one
This one is weary
And knows too much sorrow

Give me a face full of laughter
Give me a face singing songs
Give me a face giving kisses
Give me a face that belongs

Take the face that has hardened
The one with the weight of the world
The one with bags and the circles
The one with the zits and the scars

Take the face
That is breaking out
In tears
Again

Hindsight

This face I've worn for a while
And some days it feels like a mask
Somebody please take it off me
Or tell me to go back to bed

Tomorrow I hope will be different
Tomorrow I might be okay
Tomorrow I just might remember
My passion, my path, and my Way

The light in the sky will be dawning
And tomorrow will soon be today
I hope that tomorrow my face fits
And that I can sleep, if I may

Blue Moon

What's in a Name

If you could tell any version of yourself a story, what story would you tell?

"Well, that's stupid," Sam muttered to their phone.

"What's stupid?" David asked.

"Nothing, just a writing prompt that appeared on my feed."

"Ah."

Sam curled into David's side, enjoying the warmth of his arm around them. They scrolled down on their phone, but their mind kept returning to the prompt.

What story would you tell?

There was only one story worth telling, but . . . No, no, no, they were taking a break tonight. They were going to check email and scroll through social media. They had been working too hard lately, and they didn't need to write something else.

What story would you tell?

They sighed and sat up. "Hey, love, I'm going to be in my office for a bit."

David nodded absently, still watching some cooking show.

Sam stood and walked down the hall. They stepped into the tiny, closet-like room they called their office. There was barely space for a narrow desk and a small bookcase. They switched on the light and pressed the start button on the laptop, trying to gather their thoughts as it booted. When the desktop came up they sat in their old, creaking office chair and opened a new Word document.

Now comes the part where I stare blankly at the computer, Sam thought, glaring at the page before them. *How the hell do I start this, anyway?*

They slipped their headphones on, clicking over to their music player. What to listen to? A click and a song streamed into their ears. They bobbed their head in time with the melody, waiting for the words to flow out of their fingers and onto the keyboard before them. One song, then another. Nothing felt right. They typed and deleted several things, frustrated, searching.

This was the hardest part — starting something new.

"How's it coming, hon?" David asked, stepping into the

doorway.

Concentration broken, they sighed. "It's not going great, not yet."

He nodded. "I'll let you get back to it. Want coffee?"

They waved a hand, already not paying attention. "Sure, whatever."

As David left the room a hard rock song blared through Sam's headphones. They tried again to find the place within them where the words came from.

"How the hell do I say this?" No answer came from the empty doorway.

The end of one song, the beginning of another. Drums beating, a piano playing singular notes, a voice, almost a cappella. Not the most cheerful song, but it was what they needed. They put their hands back over the keys and started to type.

The moment they were born, they were given a name.

They only asked if they could change it once when they were seven. Their parents laughed at them and said no. They didn't ask again. They bought a notebook with their allowance and started to write down names. They started to write stories.

"The names are for the stories," they would lie when people asked.

Sometimes the names did go into the stories and they

would cross that name out. Sometimes the names started to feel wrong. But some names stayed, and these they kept. The names they kept went from notebook to notebook.

Their fingers were flying now, the words pouring onto the page. Typos were ignored. Words were left out entirely. Sentences ran on. They would come back to the mistakes later. The first draft was always terrible, they knew. As long as the content was good, it would all work out eventually.

They saw David come in, heard him say something, but the words washed over them without making sense. They were fully engrossed now. They lived where the words came from. Everything was music. Not the music they were listening to, they couldn't even hear it anymore. The music of their soul sang around them, pouring from their heart onto the empty page.

Memories rifled through and left behind. What were the important ones?

A locker room, middle school. Discomfort, repressed. They were where they were supposed to be, but it felt wrong. That question they kept asking themself, almost asked out loud. This wasn't the time or place. There was never a time or place to ask. Their dad didn't want to hear it. Their mom wouldn't understand.

Quietly they asked, Am I trans? No . . . no, that wasn't it.

Hindsight

But it was . . . and it wasn't . . . They ignored the laughter in their ears. They couldn't ignore the increasing discomfort. They pushed it down. It would fade in time.

It always did.

They finished dressing and closed the locker. Someone passing them shoved them into it and laughed when they almost fell.

"Freak!" someone hooted. There was more laughter and this time it had a direction. They tried to ignore it and pushed away from the lockers. They picked up their bag off the bench. They left the locker room and walked to math. There was no point in fighting back. It would only encourage them, and besides . . .

They were right.

Sam stared into space again, lost in memories. There was a lot they'd forgotten. How many times had that happened? It hurt to remember. But it was important to who they had been, who they were, and who they were becoming. They took a sip of their cold coffee. When had David brought that in?

Their playlist stopped and then started over again. They tried to collect their thoughts and leaned back over the keyboard. There was more to write. They hadn't written half of it yet.

"I'm going to bed," David said from the doorway.

"Uh-huh," Sam grunted. "Be in later."

That was a lie and they both knew it. He'd left them coffee. They were so engrossed in writing by now they could easily be up all night working. Again. It would hardly be the first time. Out of their periphery, they saw the light in the hall go out but their attention was on the page in front of them.

They sat under a tree alone. They were usually alone. They had "friends," or at least people who tolerated them. Those people didn't really get it. That group would fall silent and stare every time they tried to say something. They couldn't seem to do anything right anymore.

There had been a time during summer school when they thought they had fit in. But they hadn't been able to find those people again during the regular school year. They just didn't fit anywhere . . . They were a freak. They always had been and they always would be. No one wanted them around.

Under a cloth bracer was a thin line of scab. They had gotten scared, hadn't cut deep enough. They would try again, maybe that night, or in a few days. But they—

"Hey!" a cheerful voice interrupted. They looked up from their introspection to find two boys walking towards them. "We were in English together this summer, right?"

They nodded mutely, too afraid to speak.

The boy grinned. "Do you remember me? I'm Arthur, this is

Greg. What are you doing, eating alone?"

"I—" they started, but before they could do more than stammer out that, Arthur was giving them a hand up, and Greg was taking their backpack.

"Come eat with us!" Greg said, and Arthur slung an arm around their shoulders.

That day they ate shyly with their summer friends. The next day Arthur met them at the tree, and they were carried off.

A few days later, they removed the bracer and did not need to wear it again.

Sam fingered their wrist, remembering a wound that had left an invisible scar. Not on their body, but on their mind. Did Arthur and Greg realize what they had done that day? They should look those two up again.

They took a sip of their cold coffee, not tasting it. They remembered that night long ago. They had been left home alone. Reaching into the kitchen drawer. Sixteen years old.

So it was, for far too many like them.

They knew the statistics now. It didn't exactly help, knowing what they had gone through was almost normal . . . but they had gotten lucky, and they knew it. If they hadn't made those friends the summer before . . . If those friends hadn't found them that day . . . If those friends hadn't kept trying . . .

"Is this even a story I should tell?" The computer in front of them didn't answer. They sighed and thought of their sixteen-year-old self finding this story. "Yes, then. Okay."

They bent back over the keyboard. What else would they want that lost teenager to know? What else was there to say?

Only a few years before, a music festival of some kind. Their friend Sadie was having a conversation they hadn't been paying attention to. Just a word, that was all they heard. One word was enough. Their world turned itself upside down, then righted again.

They grabbed her arm. "Say that again. Tell me what that is. Gender fluid?"

They never could remember her words later, but it had been like lightning striking. They almost cried. They weren't alone. They weren't a freak. The relief must have shown on their face because Sadie hugged them tightly.

"Thank you," they whispered to her. "It's just . . . you just helped me find a piece of me."

"I'm glad you found it."

It had been like being hit with a brick, they reflected. Well, not a brick . . . but they had felt almost concussed afterward. They took a sip of their coffee, magically hot, and frowned at the cup. It was hot again? They looked up to see David smiling at them from the doorway, still in his pajamas. He took a sip of his own coffee. Sam glanced down at the laptop. It was almost four in the morning.

"How'd it go?" David asked. "You were up all night again."

They laughed. "So I was. I'm almost done. Thanks for the coffee, love." They smiled briefly at him before turning back to the computer. There was just one more thing to add.

The most important thing.

"Hi, how can I help you?" the barista asked.

"Um, just some light roast today," they answered, clutching the notebook tight to their chest.

"Sure." He passed over the coffee. "Can I get you anything else?"

They hesitated and took a deep breath. "Maybe a croissant?"

"Can I get your name? Did you want it warm?"

The moment of truth. They opened the notebook, the list of crossed-out names. They squinted at the next one.

"S-sam," they stammered out uncertainly. "And yes."

He wrote it on the pastry bag. "Sam today, huh? How does it feel?"

The two of them had nearly the same conversation every

day. Sometimes they wished for more, but . . . well.

They smiled, a little more assured. "I think I like it. I might put it in for a two-day trial."

He smiled. "I think it suits you, Sam. Are you still liking it?"

"We'll find out tomorrow, won't we, David?" they asked.

A few minutes later they heard the name they were testing and walked forward to collect the warm pastry. David handed them the bag with a wink. They blinked, then looked at the bag.

Sam.

Yeah, that name. It felt kind of nice. And, underneath the name, a phone number and a heart. That was even nicer.

"Sam, I'm going to work now," David said from the doorway, pulling on his shirt. "Take a nap or something, okay? You can pick it up later."

"I'm done, or almost," they said with a smile. They were kneeling in front of the bookcase, looking through the old notebooks. "Aha!"

They reached over and pulled one out. The oldest. It was tattered, worn, the back cover was missing, and it had been bent in half at least once, but Sam laid a fond hand on it. There were stories in there, but the old graphite was illegible in places. They flipped to the front page and squinted at the faded, childish writing. It was hard to read, but . . . not impossible.

"What did you find?" David stepped into the office. Sam showed him the faded page, and he squinted at it. "Names . . . ? Oh! It's on there!"

They laughed. "Yeah. I should have known sooner." They set the notebook down on the desk, still open, and yawned. "Goodness, I'm tired. I didn't realize."

David kissed their cheek. "Get some sleep. I'll see you after my shift, okay?" The two of them walked from the room, leaving behind the open notebook of names. Most of them were crossed out or faded away, but five were still readable in the early morning light.

Sasha
Parker
Taylor
Jackie
Sam

Can I Wear A Suit?

I don't feel like I can go
Unless I wear a mask
I know should just say something
But I'm afraid to ask
You always loved my style
You always loved my flare
You never seemed that ruffled
Or bothered by my hair
It's hard enough to go through this
Without needing to say
"Please do not call me by
<My deadname> today"
You never said my real name
And that makes me very sad
I probably should have said something
In the time we had
They said that it upset you
And I should have told them 'no'
I know there's nothing I can do
About it now, and so
I'm not a boy, I'm not a girl
Maybe the point is moot
But I never did like dresses
So can I just wear a suit?

I Never Heard You Say It

If everybody in the world
Someday knows my name
It will not make up for this
It will not be the same
I never heard you say it
And it makes me very sad
But they told me not to talk to you
And now I wish I had
"This is not important
Don't be selfish, don't be you"
I don't think that they understand
What that put me through
You had always told me
That I should always be myself
And in your final illness
I put me on a shelf
I'm trying to keep going
I'm trying to move on
But I never heard you say it
And now, suddenly, you're gone
Maybe I won't keep this one
I might find something new
But I never heard you say it
And I don't know what to do

Half Jack

"Half underwater, I'm half my mother's daughter"
The only half that she can ever see
Never mind about the rest, the other half
That makes the whole of me
She thinks the other half is his fault somehow
And that might actually be a fact
He's been more understanding of what I am
The half of me that's Jill, the half of me that's Jack
There's a part of me that's neither
That hides from all the noise
That doesn't understand the fuss
Of who is girls and who is boys
If she would just ask questions
She might understand
But it's not a simple matter of
Am I woman, am I man?
A part of me is wrong
It's wonder that I relate so much
To this raucous song
I don't think she'll listen
It's not what I have or what I lack
It's a part of me is Jill
But the louder part is Jack

Hindsight

Beaver Moon

The Moon and the Void

"My name is Eleena," the girl said as she thrust an apple into his empty hands. "Mama says you're a god, so I thought I would give you my apple."

He blinked up at her. She was a young child, perhaps seven or eight years old. She grinned down at him from behind mud matted hair. She was missing two teeth and her clothes were as filthy as her hair.

"What happened to your face?" he asked, setting aside the question of the apple and his godhood for a moment.

The girl scowled. "Ferth," she said sulkily, as though that explained everything.

"Eleena!" a woman called from the road. "Come away from

there!"

She grimaced. "I have to go." She raced back towards the road leaving the apple in his dumbfounded hands.

"You didn't eat the apple," she said the next day. She was clean this time, though still bruised. She was frowning at him.

He looked down at the red fruit in his hand. He had, in truth, been waiting for her to return for it. He hadn't moved since she had given it to him. She took the apple out of his hand, and put a small loaf of bread there instead.

"You eat that," she ordered. "I'll eat the apple." She sat beside him at the mouth of the cave and took a small bite.

"Where are your parents?" he asked, troubled that she was alone.

"Papa's working in the fields. Mama's cleaning and wanted me out," she said. "I have to go home soon and do my chores. I have to help milk the cows and Mama is teaching me to spin. I wanted to make sure you had something to eat today. Why aren't you eating? Aren't you hungry?"

He contemplated the difficulty of explaining to a small child that he wanted to die and looked down at the bread instead.

"It is burnt," he observed. Eleena squirmed and he glanced over at her. "Did you bake this?"

" . . . yes," she said, sounding uncomfortable. "Mama said if

I was going to burn it I was going to eat it and I can't eat anything else until it's gone . . . but it's too hard. It hurts my mouth." She sniffled.

He weighed his desire to die against her unhappiness and calmly took a bite of the hard, burnt bread.

"It is good," he told her.

She stared up at him. "You shouldn't lie even if it's to make people feel better. That's what the priest says."

He smiled. It was difficult. When was the last time he had smiled? "It is good bread. I can taste the heart and hope you put into it."

She nodded vigorously, smiling. "I wanted to make it for you! And then I burned it . . . " Her smile twisted into a pout.

He put a gentle hand on her head. "You are learning. Be patient with yourself. And next time, try not to burn the bread."

She smiled widely, missing teeth and all. "Thanks!" She rose, kissed his cheek, and ran off into the woods, presumably towards home.

"Ferth?" he asked two years later when she handed him another small loaf of bread.

Her baking had improved and this one was not burnt. She visited him often, nearly every day. All too often sporting bruises inflicted by the mysterious Ferth. She had another black eye, along with a variety of other bruises on her face and arms.

"Ferth . . . and Father," she said, looking uncomfortable. "For fighting with Ferth again." She sat next to him in the mouth of the cave and leaned against him.

He touched a gentle hand to her hair. "You should not fight as often as you do, Eleena," he said, thinking she had grown much in the last year. She was nine, almost ten now. Where had the time gone?

"He fought me first," she grumbled. "I just finished the fight he started."

"You are getting too old to be fighting like this," he chided gently. "Is there nothing you two can agree on?"

" . . . we agree that we don't want to get married. That's what Father wants, what Ferth's mother wants." She sounded disgusted.

He frowned. "You and Ferth fight like cats and dogs. You always have. Why would they wish you to marry?"

She shrugged. "Father says Ferth is going to be a merchant like his mother and he'll be able to provide for me. Ferth's mother thinks us fighting is cute. And the rest of the village thinks I'm weird because you're my only friend."

He considered this. He had never thought about the effect his friendship would have on her. She was getting to the age where being in the woods with strange men would tell against her. He was doing her no favors, letting her bring him bread and talk to him.

He picked up her hand and set the uneaten bread in it.

"You should stop coming here," he told her.

She looked up at him. "Why?"

He sighed. "You are old enough to know why."

She stood, scowling. "I thought you were my friend!"

"I am your friend. As your friend, I am telling you to go and live your life. Forget about me. Make friends in the village and—" She threw the bread at him and began to storm off. "The bread."

"I made it for you! Idiot." She ran into the woods, and did not return to his cave for many years.

"May I stay here?" a quiet voice asked.

He opened his eyes. He was so tired and so close to death. It was dark, long past the hour when Eleena should have been in bed. But there she stood.

He has seen her only distantly for . . . how many years had it been? They blurred together in his mind, distorted by the thousands of others. He had watched her growing taller from a distance as she passed him on the road. When had her smile disappeared? Was it recent? Or had it been the day he had told her to stay away?

"Ferth?" he asked, looking at the bruises on her face and

arms.

She laughed bitterly and sank to her knees before him, suddenly pale. "No . . . not Ferth. Father." She closed her eyes, and he saw a glitter of tears. "Please. Please."

Slowly, almost creaking, he unfolded from where he had been seated for fifteen long years. He stood and walked to where she had fallen.

"Can you stand?" he asked. "Are you hurt?"

"I'm dizzy and my head aches. I fell so many times, coming here. I'm out of strength."

He took in a little power from the darkness of the night and touched a hand to her head carefully. "You have a concussion," he told her. "Eleena, I can help you, but there is a price for the help a god might give. I— I cannot ask you to make a Bargain like this . . . "

"I will make it."

"No," he told her firmly. "I will. I will make the Bargain for your sake. When you are healed we may discuss the Bargain *you* must make but, for now, the only price paid will be mine and mine alone." He took some more power from the night and lifted her carefully into his arms. He turned and strode into the forest.

"Where are we going?" she asked.

"To my brother Dionmachus. His wife, Amara the Sky-Touched, knows of healing."

He walked for a while into the forest, calling in the power of the night. Could he bring her to Amara? Or would it be better to call Amara to her? He wasn't certain how badly she was hurt. To travel the way of the gods took a toll on mortals. Was she strong enough?

"Where are we going?" she asked again, her voice weaker.

"To my brother's wife, Amara," he repeated. "She will aide you." He stopped and shook his head. "No. No, I will need to call her here. I do not think you will survive being brought to her."

He walked a little farther into the forest, now looking for a clearing to set her down in. There, maybe. He walked into a small patch of clear ground. Moonlight broke through the trees, spilling onto her face as he set her on the soft grass.

She covered her face with a hand. "Where . . . where are we?"

"Hush," he told her. "Try to stay awake . . . " He drew her hand away from her face.

She grimaced. "The moon is too loud. Make it stop."

He chuckled. "I would not blot out Auntie Moon even for you, dear Eleena. Hush for a moment." He looked out into the forest around them, still holding her hand. He sighed. "Amara, if you can hear me, I need your help."

"You need no aide from me, brother-in-law," a quiet voice said. "You have already saved her life, as twice now she has saved yours."

Amara stepped quietly out of the shadows behind him and knelt beside him. She smoothed back Eleena's hair. Eleena blinked up at her, then looked back to the moon.

"There, little sister. Is your head feeling any better?" To him, she said, "Your mother has been screaming in my ear about you two since you picked her up. Wait till your father hears. He'll be thrilled."

He frowned at her. "What?"

"Eleena is Moon-Touched. As I am Sky-Touched," she explained patiently. She covered his and Eleena's joined hands. And he knew what she meant. "We're glad to still have you, brother-in-law. Dionmachus sends his love, his congratulations, and . . . " She smacked him in the head.

"Ow!"

She only laughed. "He sends that too. Most of your siblings send that, actually. You're lucky I am only delivering the one." She smoothed back Eleena's hair again and stood. "I'll be nearby in case you need me, but I think you had better explain what happened, and the price you'll both pay for it. It's your fault after all." She turned.

"Wait," he said. "What do you mean it's my fault?"

"Don't be silly. Where is the moon, Claec?"

And she walked into the forest.

He sat there looking down at Eleena speculatively for several moments as she blinked blankly up at the moon. Her eyes cleared at last and she sat up slowly, stiffly, as though she had lain there for years. He helped her, trying to decide what to say. What could he say? Amara was right. This was all his fault.

"I feel weird," Eleena said at last. "My head . . . It doesn't hurt anymore, but it feels sort of echoey in here."

"Like a voice filled all the spaces around you, and now all is silent." He nodded, sighing. "Yes."

She blinked at him, and then stared at her hands. "What happened? I remember being carried through the woods, and then . . . then I'm not sure."

He looked up at the dark sky, avoiding the gaze of the watchful moon. "I saved your life by accident, and more than that. I carried you and then I set you down where Auntie Moon could see."

"What are you talking about?" she asked, sounding confused.

He looked back at her and found her watching him. "I am Claec, god of the void. You saved my life, not once, but twice. The sky my Mother saw all and told it to her sister the moon. Auntie Moon saw me trying to save your life tonight. She decided to reward you." He sighed. "I am afraid you are no longer quite mortal, Eleena."

"No . . . " she said quietly. "No, I'm not, am I?" She looked up at him and smiled. "Because the void carries the moon like you carried me."

He helped her to her feet, feeling awkward. "Eleena, goddess of the moon, I . . . I promised I would pay the price for your healing, but I fear we will both pay this price."

She shook her head. "It's only a price if you make it one, Claec." She laughed. "Besides, as arranged marriages go, you're better than Ferth would have been anyway."

He smiled then, a small smile. "I would hope." His smile faded. "I am sorry. I never intended . . . and we barely know each other." He rubbed the back of his neck awkwardly. "I wanted to die before I met you, and now I must live for you."

"Hey. We've got all of forever to figure this out." She took his hand. "So, let's start. My name is Eleena and I am apparently the goddess of the moon now. I'm nineteen, and new to this whole being a goddess thing."

He smiled again, and this time it lit up his face. "My name is Claec, and I am the god of the void. I am . . . I have no idea how old I am, anymore."

"Really? I wonder if your father knows?"

"I don't think Father even knows how old *he* is anymore."

She laughed, and then looked at him seriously. "Claec . . . will you tell me why you wanted to die?"

"It started with my brother, Xefiev . . . As far too many stories do," Claec began with a sigh, and started to walk.

Still holding his hand, Eleena walked with him into the forest. Hand in hand, the god of the void walked with the goddess of the moon through the forest talking quietly.

Elsewhere in the forest Amara watched them. She smiled and disappeared into the trees.

Sing a Song of Sunshine

Sing a song of sunshine in the middle of the night
When there's nothing really wrong, but there's nothing going right
When there's clouds and mist and rain
And you're wondering once again
If you'll ever see the stars or the morning light

How Do You Write What Can't Be Written?

How do you write what can't be writ?
How do you light what can't be lit?
How do you speak what can't be spoken?
How do you fix what's beyond broken?
You took my voice away
It died there while I lay
Not dead but dying
No tears but crying
Sighing
I stopped writing
I put pen to paper and nothing came out
I was left as nothing
I was fear
I was doubt
You look in the mirror
It's been more than a year
Who am I anymore
I don't know you
You find definitions
I am this
I am not this
I am more than this
I am more than this
Please let me be more than this
More than what happened
More than what didn't
I'm losing the thread of my thoughts
I lost the rhyme
Where is the rhythm?
How do you write what can't be written?

Heartbeat

5 am
Good(?) morning
I see we're here again
Awake
Waiting for the nothing
Where something
Once was
Where someone
Once was

Empty, aching, anxious
Screaming and crying
But not
My mind rages
My body is calm
But for the pain
Where something
Once was
Where someone
Once was

I miss everyone
Anymore
I know
I'm hardly alone
Not places
Not things
People
Home is
Where the heart is
My home
Is people

Hindsight

I want
To go home
I want
To go home
Where something
Once was
Where someone
Once was

I will find
New homes
New people
Breathe in love
Breathe out pain
Over
And over
Again
And again
It's going
To hurt
Where something
Once was
Where someone
Once was

I'll try again tomorrow
I'll try again today
With the sunshine
And the sorrow
With the garden
And the home
In my heart
Where something
Once was
Where someone
Once was

Cold Moon

I'm Sorry, My Body

I'm sorry, my body, for what I have done
What we have been through, the songs you have sung
Tell me again of the crack in the night
The dislocated shoulder, the numbness, the fright
Tell me again of the pain in my head
How many times over trapped in my bed?
The seizures untended for many a year?
I will pay a price, and that price will be dear
The tendons I tore? The foot three months broken?
The spur in my heel? Other things left unspoken?
I'm sorry, my body, you deserved so much more
Than this person who also was stronger before
Pain wears away at the body, the mind
And now all that's left is what pain left behind
But even what's broken and breaking may mend
Let's try to do better in the new year, old friend

Grief

Grief is like a blister
It feels pretty weird
Kind of numb and painful
Where the damage is done
Someday this feels blister will pop
And my feelings will ooze out
Like lymph and pus
Getting everywhere
For now, I am protected
From that searing pain
By a thin layer
Of half-numb skin
I can feel the damage
I know I am hurt
Someday I will feel it
Someday I will cry
It's rushing up to meet me
For now, I only sigh
I know that I will miss you
From this day to my last
If there is a heaven
I'm sure that you are there
With Uriah and Heather
Probably wishing
I was wearing pants

Yesterday's Sorrow

After days of malaise
On a dopamine hype
I sat down to write
In a new kind of type
Words with some rhythm
Words with some rhyme
I do what I want
Most of the time
Contradict when I want to
Sing in the void
I've all fucks to give
I'm just usually annoyed
By the past and the present
My failures and fears
I can't see the future
But I hope that it clears
So here's to today
And here's to tomorrow
All new kinds of love
Fuck yesterday's sorrow

In Days of Auld Lang Syne

"Should auld acquaintance be forgot, and never brought to mind . . . " Klause sang off key.

"Bah humbug," Juno grumbled.

He threw an arm around her shoulders and ruffled her hair. "That's Christmas, Scrooge, and I'll remind you, that wasn't said by a good guy."

She smoothed down her hair again and shoved him off. "Look, I just don't see anything to celebrate about this year. Do I have to talk about all the bad shit that went down?"

"Nah." He threw his arm back around her. "If I want to see that kind of bullshit I'll watch the news."

She tried to shove him off again, with little effect. "Dude, you smell like weed. Not even good weed."

"I like the bad stuff. I offered you some."

"And I said no," she reminded him. "If I'm toking it better be worth it."

He poked her gently on the nose. "Shit's legal now."

"So buy the good stuff if you want me to smoke with you." She caught his hand as he started to poke her nose again. "And stop that."

"Come on, Juno, sing New Year's carols with me!"

"There's no such thing, Klause."

"Sure there is." And to her horror, he began to sing again. "Maybe it's just too early in the game, oh but I thought I'd ask you just the same . . . "

"Klause . . ." she said warningly.

He ignored her. "What are you doing New Year's? New Year's Eve?"

"Bah humbug."

He sighed. "What do I need to do to get some spirit out of you?"

She stood up, finally throwing off his arm, and started to pace. "Make this year suck less? Make it so I can go outside without a mask on?"

He stood and took her hands. "Look, Juno, I know this year has been rough, but it's been hard for everyone. I miss going out just as much as you do. You know me, I'm a people person!"

She did know that, but . . . "You spend half the day on Zoom now."

He poked her again on the nose before she could stop him. "And you could too. Come to the Zoom party tonight, I'll introduce you."

"I don't know . . . " she groaned. "I still don't feel like there's anything to celebrate."

He put his arm around her shoulders again, more gently this time. "Well . . . what about the end of the year? It's over, right? Isn't that worth celebrating?"

She laughed hollowly. "Feels like an empty victory. We survived, sure, but . . . "

"Sometimes you have to take what you can get," he told her gently. "Here."

He went into the kitchen and came out with two tumblers filled with sparkling apple juice. He passed her one and clinked glasses with her. "To twenty twenty one?"

"Sure." She took a sip and he drained his glass. "You were just thirsty."

"Well, yeah."

She took another drink of the cider as he flopped onto the couch. She sat down on the floor in front of him. "What do you think next year will be like?" she asked.

Klause ruffled her hair again. "Well, it's got to be better than this," he sighed.

"Yeah," she agreed, and took another sip of cider. "It's got to be."

"Still," he said. "It's not all bad. I made some good friends this year, and we got to know each other for the first time since we became roommates."

She sighed. "Yeah, I guess there is that."

"Is it enough?" He asked

She thought. "Yeah. Yeah, I guess so. To twenty-twenty-one?"

"To twenty-twenty-one. In days of auld lang syne!"

About the Author

Starting from the beginning, my name is Eli Kwake, pronounced iˈlaɪ kwāk. I am pansexual, polyamorous, and genderqueer. My pronouns are they/them. I am a musician, an artist, a writer, a drag king, a lover, a spouse, a friend, a foe, a human, a dragon. I make no apologies for who and what I am. I was forged in fire. I am bigger on the inside. It's nice to meet you.
You can find me on Twitter: @EliKwake
https://www.elikwake.com

Kickstarter Supporters

In no particular order

Heather Snitch
Kathryn
Bitterblue
Jason Fuhrman
Joel Rieck
AmCat
Gregory Lemon
Ashe
Tillerz
Lisa Schubert May
Kasia Szczerbinski
Linda Johanna Costello
Abi Pullen
Chrissy Mackey, PhD
Mother of Bunnies
Pride Ascending
Danielle Mitchell
Greg Schneider
Aaron Wingo

Rachyl Whitney
Sarah Lemler
Jessica Hunter
Stephanie M
Erika Page
Kat Schulz-Booth
BasicDragon
Sergey Kochergan
K.S. Bishoff
Stephen S. Farbman
Amélie S
Stephanie Gildart
Ghislaine Sopher-Phillips
Lethann Aeda
Mama Ruth
Katherine Panowicz
Amanda Palmer
Nik Fenmore
Amanda Hogue

CPSIA information can be obtained
at www.ICGtesting.com
Printed in the USA
BVHW092157060521
606682BV00002B/119